POEMS IN PERSONS

An Introduction to the Psychoanalysis of Literature

Books by Norman N. Holland

The First Modern Comedies
The Shakespearean Imagination
Psychoanalysis and Shakespeare
The Dynamics of Literary Response
Poems in Persons

POEMS IN PERSONS

An Introduction to the Psychoanalysis of Literature

NORMAN N. HOLLAND

W · W · NORTON & COMPANY · INC ·
NEW YORK

FIRST EDITION

Library of Congress Cataloging in Publication Data
Holland, Norman Norwood, 1927–
  Poems in persons.
  Includes bibliographical references.
  1. Psychoanalysis and literature.   2. Poetry.
I. Title.
PN56.P92H6   801' .92   73–4691
ISBN 0–393–01099–6

1 2 3 4 5 6 7 8 9 0

To Katie and John

Contents

Preface

IT HAS BEEN my ambition for a long time to write a short book, to give my own readers that feeling of ease and mastery with which I pick up a slim volume as against the sense of impending trouble the heavy tome induces. Now, happily, I can feel that I have done so and hope that that very brevity will guarantee a clear and forthright introduction to some major breakthroughs in the understanding of literature and of ourselves.

In the same breath, however, I must admit that this brief book could not have come into being were it not for the two rather more weighty treatises from which it derives: *The Dynamics of Literary Response* (New York: Oxford University Press, 1968) and *5 Readers Reading* (in preparation). Without their lengthy development of the relationships among literary works and readers and writers, I could not now write this brief introduction. Similarly, because those books exist, or at least *Dynamics*, I have felt free to rest on its statements of certain issues. This introduction, therefore, says nothing at all about evaluation and next to nothing about literary characters. Again, instead of trying to cover a range of literary materials, I have built this book around lyric poems and occurrences of one particular fantasy: the unconscious wish to undo, either lovingly or hostilely, one's separateness from a nurturing other. This fantasy serves multiply and economically for an introduction, because it touches on the relation of literary works to human beings in at least three different ways.

In this book, as in the experimental work from which it

derives, I am indebted to the Research Foundation of the State
University of New York for a series of grants that have assisted
not only in this particular study but in the development at
Buffalo of a major center for the psychological study of literature. Betty Jane Saik has graced these projects and also the
chapters that follow with her administrative and secretarial
skills, for which I express my profoundest respect and grati-
tude. The free atmosphere of my department and its openness
to new kinds of literary studies have made possible a professional exploration and personal growth that conventional disci-
plinary boundaries quite prevent and for which I am deeply
grateful. The comments of my colleagues in the Buffalo Group
for Applied Psychoanalysis and its sponsoring organization, the
Center for the Psychological Study of the Arts, have helped
me more than I can possibly write down. I am also grateful to
City Lights Books for permission to reprint "The Day Lady
Died" by Frank O'Hara and to Norman Holmes Pearson,
H.D.'s friend and literary executor, not only for permission to
reprint some of her prose and poetry but for many unusual
generosities both as scholar and as copyright owner.

I am happy to have been able to present these three chapters separately as lectures and articles to literary and psychoanalytic audiences. Each of these presentations has afforded me,
in its own way, some of that precious give and take which en-
genders and nourishes intellectual discovery, and I have indicated my several indebtednesses in the notes to the separate
chapters. More generally, both I and this book owe more than
any footnotes can indicate to the intelligence and vision of two
younger scholars in this field. Murray Schwartz has used his
extraordinary range of reading to alert me to a number of
theoretical and therapeutic issues I would have missed. David
Bleich, by gently but persistently questioning my basic assump-
tions, has worked a major shift in my understanding of subjectivity.

This book, however, as a quick, brief contribution to the miniature, belongs to Katie and John, even as the days of your smallness rush past, lingering only in parental photographs and memories. May this book last long enough to serve you (and its other readers) as one introduction among many to the great adventure which is the poem in every person.

NORMAN N. HOLLAND

POEMS IN PERSONS

An Introduction to the
Psychoanalysis of Literature

Prologue

PEOPLE are the natural habitat of literature. A literary work completely separate from any human mind may be possible, but, by that very definition, we can never know or care about it. The literary work, in this context, is subjective.

We accept this subjectivity in the making of literature, for example, in the familiar idea that literature is self-expression. The style, we agree, is the man himself, although we often seem a bit hazy as to just how that self appears in what he writes. Usually, studies of a writer's "life and works" relate the two only in the most general way, although occasionally they run to the opposite extreme, yoking isolated details from the work to real or supposed experiences in life by violent and forced inferences. This book will suggest ways of finding calmer and more pervasive continuities between the writer's creations and his personality.

When we talk of the reading of literature, however, not its creation but its re-creation, many people become distinctly uneasy at the idea of finding self-expression or personal style or subjectivity in the literary experience. We would like that experience to be "objective" even though a few minutes' conversation after any theatrical performance shows how differently people felt about it, and more often than not one finds equally skillful critics differing in their interpretations and analysis. Certainly, the ever-growing body of critical and scholarly literature offers little hope that even highly trained professional readers of accepted classics will soon arrive at any "objective" consensus. As we shall see, the dynamics by which people experience literature reveals a highly subjective re-creation, and, in a way, the real puzzle is not why people react differently to the same work, but how they could ever share the same response. And behind this purely literary problem lurk larger philosophical and psychological questions.

Like every human experience, literature has both something subjective in it and something objective. If we treat "objective" and "subjective" as two neat little boxes and insist on sorting aspects of experience into one or the other, we shall have no way of accounting for literary creation or re-creation, or all the other kinds of total experience that combine the two. To be sure, just as the tree does vibrate the air in the forest even if no one is there to hear it fall, so there is an "objective" literary text. And one could argue with equal cogency that there is neither noise of falling tree nor literature unless there is also an experiencer who creates them as his own private and subjective experiences which no one else can share or even know. But it is quite arbitrary to insist on these extreme positions. Really, subjectivity and objectivity lie along a kind of win-here-lose-there continuum. The more objective you are, the more removed from pure experience; the more subjective, the more you lose sight of and distort the objective reality. Finally, "objective reality" and "pure experience" are themselves only useful fictions, vanishing points we approach but never reach.

The problem, then, is not to sort out subjective from objective but to see how the two combine when we have experiences. A poem—I shall use poems as paradigms for literary experiences generally—a poem, taken purely objectively, is nothing but specks of carbon black on dried wood pulp. If it is written in a script I do not understand (Arabic, say, or Chinese), I cannot tell a poem from a table of logarithms, a bill of lading, or a manual of instructions. Yet a poem, unlike those other writings, allows many people to experience it intensely, and, of course, it results from some intense subjective experience in its maker's mind. A poem can get "into" a personality, or, more exactly, readers and writers use poems to engage their own mental processes so fully they can even lose all sense of themselves as such. But how?

That is finally a psychological question, and this book sets out the answers modern psychoanalytic psychology offers. They are fairly sophisticated answers, based on rather recent trends in psychoanalysis. Nevertheless, I have been able to keep this book an "introduction" by not presuming on any prior psychological background. Chapter I studies the mind of one particular poet to reveal the relation between poetic style and total personality—identity, if you will. The second chapter uses a poem (by that poet) to compare the personalities and experiences of two people reading it. Chapter II probes the private experience: reading as the re-creation of a poem through one's unique lifestyle or, again, identity. The third chapter explores the ways these personal experiences can be shared and private readings become communal ones in, for example, criticism or the teaching of literature.

Because these last sentences have phrasings like "Chapter I studies" or "The third chapter explores," they remind me that I, like many literary critics, have gotten the habit of hiding behind a polite fiction, namely, that books do things to people, and critics merely witness their actions like innocent bystanders. The convention is so common, you probably would not have noticed the misplaced concreteness had I not paused to point it out. Many, perhaps most critics write, not as though they themselves were actively discovering forms and synthesizing ideas in what they read, but as if they were just passively reporting what is "objectively" there.

This modest, self-effacing convention, however, obscures precisely the question we are exploring: how a person's personality affects what he writes and reads. I shall therefore adopt a style in writing this book in which I do not assume automatically that I am privy to incontrovertible truths about the text. I shall be frank with "I" or "you" or "we" when the event I am talking about depends on the specific and unique way my mind or yours has constructed it, and I shall use "one" or "people" to generalize about human beings only when I really mean *everybody*. You may be surprised, as I was, to see how frequently the personal pronouns are required and how they clarify, sometimes quite drastically, issues like subjectivity and objectivity.

ONE

A Maker's Mind

WE CAN BEGIN where the poem begins—in the mind of its maker. Or we could if talking about writers did not send the discourse soaring on one of the most magical catchwords of all time, creativity. As long ago as Plato's *Ion*, creativity had taken on the aura of a divine madness, and even today psychologists study it as they would a disease like obesity or alcoholism. That is, they convene a group of people with the syndrome and then try to find some other traits they have in common which will support a formula of explanation. Creative people can "regress in the service of the ego." When shown two pictures, they tend to prefer the more complicated one. They create in order to "reconstitute" persons and things they have destroyed in their aggressive fantasies. Artists and poets, at least by the lavender light of late nineteenth-century Romanticism, are *maudits:* neurotic, homosexual, or downright mad. Even in the colder light of twentieth-century tests, artists and writers describe telepathic and supernatural experiences more often than "normal" people, have scarier dreams, and resort more to infantile or "primary process" thinking.

Common sense, however, suggests that the odds are against finding a single magical faculty called "creativity" possessed by artists and writers. After all, who decided the word applied only to those in the arts? Surely scientists, statesmen, engineers, publishers, or publicans can all be "creative." Once we recognize that the word applies beyond the arts, however, it very quickly becomes so general as to mean little more than "adaptive." What then are the tests testing?

Even within the arts, "creativity" does not seem a useful level at which to generalize, because the created product is so individual. Adding up traits and averaging away individuality will tell us those abilities helpful to all writers (a good memory, for example, or agility at typing); but averaging will be just the wrong way to learn why *this* writer writes or why he writes the way he does. If we do not think those the crucial questions, then we are replacing the originality that made us wonder about creativity in the first place with the mere common denominator of writing.

Paradoxically, then, I think we can learn more about creativity in general by studying one creative person in depth, and the function creativity plays in his singular psyche, than by studying multitudes. But how can we know a poet's or novelist's mind except tautologically—by the very poems and fantasies whose creation we want to explain? We can't—with one unique exception: H.D.

I

Books of literary history relegate H.D., much too automatically, I think, to the Imagist movement. To be sure, she was one of its founders, a kind of stalking-horse for Ezra Pound, to whom she was briefly engaged. In 1913, Pound called for poems "austere, direct, free from emotional slither," "presentation, not representation," "direct treatment of the 'thing' whether subjective or objective," a style which, as we shall see, Hilda Doolittle had to find singularly congenial. In it she made her first poetic successes, and because of them Pound awarded her her literary sobriquet: he sent off her poems to be published with the signature, "H.D., Imagiste."

OREAD

Whirl up, sea—
whirl your pointed pines,
splash your great pines
on our rocks,
hurl your green over us,
cover us with your pools of fir.

(1914)

STORM

You crash over the trees,
you crack the live branch—
the branch is white,
the green crushed,
each leaf is rent like split wood.

You burden the trees
with black drops,
you swirl and crash—
you have broken off a weighted leaf
in the wind,
it is hurled out,
whirls up and sinks,
a green stone.

(1915) [1]

The way an ocean swirl can look like green needles of fir, the way I have seen a leaf caught in the wind plummet like a stone —H.D. presents images without representing them. Yet in the very act of giving me in words a reality supposedly objective, she presents her subjective concerns as well. In particular, she fuses green waves with green pines or shows how the destroying sea of "Storm" transmutes leaves into wood or stone. Associated with these fusions and mergers are words like "crack," "crash," "crushed," or "broken," and, with them, the use of commas as sentence markers, leading me to a sense of incantatory uncertainty as to where we are in the development of the poem.

Pure Imagism, as such, quickly disappeared in a larger poetic quest, although its anti-Victorian demand for precision in thought and image became a cornerstone for all later Anglo-American poetry. However, H.D. did not cease with Imagism either as poet or as Hilda Doolittle's signature. Over the next four decades, as Joseph N. Riddel has shown, she moved away from naive objectivity toward more awareness of language and myth, finally into a highly self-conscious concept of the poem as a voyaging into the unknown territory of its—and her—own creating.[2] No one, in English, has more subtly or more relentlessly sought to body forth a self in the hieroglyphs of myth, dream, and image than she; "mysteries" she called them in the poem with which she concluded her 1931 volume, *Red Roses for Bronze:*

> The mysteries remain
> I keep the same
> cycle of seed-time
> and of sun and rain;
> Demeter in the grass,
> I multiply,
> renew and bless
> Iacchus in the vine;
> I hold the law,
> I keep the mysteries true,
> the first of these
> to name the living, dead;
> I am red wine and bread.
>
> *I keep the law,*
> *I hold the mysteries true,*

I am the vine,
the branches, you
and you.

She is probably, after Emily Dickinson, America's greatest woman poet, although it is her misfortune to be read in the shadow of a generation of giants—Eliot, Pound, Stevens, Williams, and the rest.

For someone studying the creative mind, however, the singular importance of H.D. lies not in her poems (or her fiction and essays) but in one unique source of insight she has left us, her account of her analysis with Freud.[3] I know of no account by an analysand that tells more about Freud, his techniques, or the analytic experience as it seems from within. Written in 1944, it was based on a diary she had kept during the analysis, but she left the diary in Switzerland during World War II and hence did not use it during the actual writing. Anyway, *Tribute to Freud* does not move chronologically or treat their relationship as a case history. It is a series of memories in free association, and details about Freud and his technique as a therapist mingle with the visions and themes of H.D.'s own life. Yet, with a little persistence, a little reading between the lines, one can unscramble her reminiscences to give an absolutely unparalleled picture of the infantile forces that engendered a poet's life pattern, including the fact of her writing and, indeed, the very style of her writing. "I have often had the fancy," wrote Yeats, "that there is some one Myth for every man, which, if we but knew it, would make us understand all he did and thought." [4] With this one poet, H.D., such an understanding becomes possible.

We can begin to develop H.D.'s myth with a phrase Horace Gregory quotes from H.D. herself, that her concern was "a wish to make real to myself what is most real" or (again in H.D.'s words) to "re-dedicate our gifts to spiritual realism." [5] The tension in a phrase like "spiritual realism" or the paradox of a "most real" which must be made real illustrates the polarities or oxymora from which her poetry builds: hot—cold; fertile—salt; blunt—pointed; dark—bright; soft—hard; fire-as-passion—fire-as-destruction; new—old; male—female; passion—reason, and the rest. As in this passage from "Toward the Piraeus" (1922):

> If I had been a boy,
> I would have worshipped your grace,
> I would have flung my worship
> before your feet,
> I would have followed apart,
> glad, rent with an ecstasy
> to watch you turn
> your great head, set on the throat,
> thick, dark with its sinews,
> burned and wrought
> like the olive stalk,
> and the noble chin
> and the throat.
>
> I would have stood,
> and watched and watched
> and burned,
> and when in the night,
> from the many hosts, your slaves,
> and warriors and serving men
> you had turned
> to the purple couch and the flame
> of the woman, tall like the cypress tree
> that flames sudden and swift and free
> as with crackle of golden resin
> and cones and the locks flung free
> like the cypress limbs,

bound, caught and shaken and loosed,
bound, caught and riven and bound
and loosened again,
as in rain of a kingly storm
or wind full from a desert plain.
So, when you had risen
from all the lethargy of love and its heat,
you would have summoned me,
me alone,
and found my hands,
beyond all the hands in the world,
cold, cold, cold,
intolerably cold and sweet.

I find in this poem, among other contrasts, male and female, passion and worship, many and one, heat and cold, but to me the most basic of all, in this as in the rest of her poems, is between the small, precise, and named and the huge, abstract, and blank, between the boy's cold hand and the flaming, storming hero, like the contrast between the leaf and the scarcely named "Storm" in the Imagist lyric.

I find the same tension in her formal style: short, un-rhymed lines usually in small, two-line stanzaic structures but set in poems placeless, timeless, structureless. I see the same polarity in her imagery. A flower is rarely just a flower with H.D.: it is a rose or a violet or a lily or a gentian or a plum-blossom. Naming and precision give power, strength, and reality. Trees, types of rock, buildings, colors—all are set out with the exactitude Pound admired. The body itself occurs in defined body-parts (as above, feet, chin, throat), while it is difficult for H.D. to show us a whole person—or personality. Men are hard and armored, while women who yield to men dissolve into flowers, rocks, or water, like the flaming, riven cypress-woman:

how reconcile

the magnetic steel-clad Achilles
with the flowering pomegranate? [6]

Yet, despite this pattern—or because of it—I often, in her
dramatic monologues, cannot tell whether the speaker is male
or female.

H.D.'s strength lies in her rendition of detail. I rarely feel,
however, that she succeeds in structuring those details into a
poetic, dramatic, or still more acutely, fictional whole. Poems,
fiction, even essays like *Tribute to Freud* or *By Avon River*
become a series of isolated images or events linked by free
associations, often through mythological themes. At the very
sentence level, her boundaries tend to be ill-defined. Verbs
take indeterminate forms. A sentence modifier from one sentence will seem to apply to the next. Lists, of which H.D. uses
many, will be oddly broken between sentences. The word to
which a pronoun or adjective refers may be one or two sentences back; the reference itself may be twinned or multiple.
Often, for structure, she will resort to a series of parallel structures to be summed into a totality. Sometimes, she will use
negations—a series of *not*'s or *nor*'s to strip off the extraneous
and come to the final, finely rendered residue as a climax. At
other times, she will polarize the poem into extremes, like the
flaming woman and the cold boy.

No doubt, H.D. sought out myths partly to use them as
organizing forms. If one can see present people, events, and
feelings as projections or continuations of a simpler, more
structured, mythic past, they become more manageable and,
for H.D. at least, somehow more real. She uses for living people the image of a palimpsest or a series of old photographic
negatives on top of one another—the sign one sees on the surface implies a deeper reality underneath.[7] She seeks to turn
herself, her very body, into an hieroglyph or emblem [8]—as in

the use of her initials for a seal or sign. Her poetry, like the myths she emulates, manifests that which is spiritual, abstract, and timeless by the hard, the real, the objective, the exact.

We can use as first statements of the "H.D.-myth" Thomas B. Swann's generalizations: he speaks of "escape into the hard impersonality of nature" and her "merging with the hard, changeless integrity of the natural world." [9] Joseph N. Riddel points out, "H.D.'s images of the real invariably accentuate the manifest 'shape' of subjectivity, of inwardness objectified and hence rendered in the universal shape of art." The world of the early poems, he shows,

is a world of cold, hard beauty, occasionally threatened by the softness of decay or the oppressiveness of a suffocating heat; a world, that is, of willed objectivity which barely conceals the inwardness that reminds the self of its imminent nothingness. The objectivity of H.D.'s world is a kind of ultimate subjectivity.[10]

Now, can we reach from those critical *aperçus* to the personality of the poet and the origins of H.D.'s creative power? We can, by means of that extraordinary document, her memoir of her analysis.

II

The story of H.D. and Freud begins in 1915, the year H.D. lost her first child through a miscarriage. Daughter of a distinguished astronomer, "who seldom even at table focused upon anything nearer, literally, than the moon," [11] and a mother who seems to have been equally abstracted, she was the one girl among five brothers, one of whom, Gilbert, the one just older than she, was not only her mother's admitted favorite but someone with whom H.D. herself identified. In 1915 she was twenty-nine, her poetry just coming to be recognized. Two years earlier, she had married her fellow-Imagist, Richard Aldington, but he had left to fight in France when the war broke out. "From shock and repercussions of war news broken to me in a rather brutal fashion," she lost her first child. Her autobiographical novels, *Palimpsest* (1926) and *Bid Me to Live* (1960), imply that sometime during this period, Aldington took a mistress, perhaps during the pregnancy itself. At any rate, their marriage broke up in 1919 (though, interestingly, she does not discuss or even mention this in *Tribute to Freud*).

In 1918 her favorite brother was killed in action in France; her father died a year later from the stroke he suffered at the news. At the end of 1919, she was sick with double pneumonia and awaiting the birth of her second child, determined that this child would live. Perdita (so her mother named her) did live, but H.D. herself went into a "nervous breakdown," [12] perhaps a post-partum depression. The poetess Bryher (pen-name of the wealthy Winifred Ellerman) rescued her, taking her to Greece to recover. While there, H.D. had an hallucination or mystical vision of extraordinary intensity. As she describes it in the memoir, it was not frightening to her, though she felt it as occult and so described it to Freud in the analysis many years later. He, however, singled this vision out as "the most dangerous or the only actually dangerous 'symptom.' "

H.D.'s relationship with Bryher continued even after the latter's marriage to Robert McAlmon, who told "of long train trips about the continent with the two women quarreling in the compartment driving him nearly insane." William Carlos Williams said H.D. had some part in the marriage's final "disastrous outcome" and the McAlmons' separation and divorce,[13] and (Norman Holmes Pearson, H.D.'s long-time friend and literary executor, tells me) McAlmon "broke with Bill Wms on this." Pearson describes H.D. as "passionately heterosexual," and Freud, in H.D.'s account, did not single out anything relating to homosexuality as part of her psychic life, although he had read *Palimpsest* before meeting H.D., and the

document that has been written upon several times

autobiographical sections of this novel at least raise the issue. Given Freud's theories in 1933, the loss of self-object boundaries in the mystical vision would have seemed of more moment to him, anyway.

It is not too clear exactly what motivated H.D. herself to seek therapy—this symptom or (more likely) the wish to free herself of "repetitive thoughts and experiences," to "take stock of my very modest possessions of mind and body," "to sort out, relive and reassemble the singular series of events and dreams that belonged in historical time, to the 1914–1919 period." In later life, she described herself to Swann as doing, in this period, "studies in . . . psychological investigation." [14] However it came about, she began "some fascinating, preliminary talks" with Hanns Sachs in Berlin, but he was leaving for America. Sachs asked her if she would consider working with "the Professor" if he would take her. She would, he did, and she began work with Freud on March 5, 1933.

Freud conducted the analysis in English (as he had often done for English and American patients after World War I). H.D. speaks of her own German as "sketchy," while Freud "was speaking English without a perceptible trace of accent." She worked with Freud "four days a week from five to six; one day, from twelve to one." They worked for "between three and four months," until Sir John Ellerman, Bryher's father, died on July 16, when H.D. seems to have left Vienna, not planning to return.[15] She did return, however, at the end of October 1934. Austria's relations with Germany were deteriorating rapidly—Dollfuss, the Chancellor, had been assassinated by Nazi revolutionaries that July—but what brought H.D. back was the news that one of the Professor's other patients, a philosopher-pilot nicknamed "the Flying Dutchman," had crashed and died in Tanganyika. This second period of analysis lasted five weeks, from the end of October 1934 to December 1, 1934, when "The war closed on us."

The relationship between H.D. and Freud differed, however, from the therapeutic or training analysis of today. A
modern analyst would want more than five months before
calling his work analysis. For Freud, five months would be
enough (for training, anyway) if "deep" material was reached,
and it is clear from H.D.'s memoir that it was. Ernest Jones, in
his brief review of her book, says quite directly, "She was
analyzed by Freud for some months in the year 1933–34."
There may be simply a question of terminology here, for
Freud himself could write, "I analyzed Mahler for an after-
noon in the year 1912." [16]

Furthermore, Freud evidently related to H.D. not only as
her training analyst but also as a teacher. "The Professor had
said in the beginning that he classed me in the same category
as the Flying Dutchman—we were students." "Seekers or
'students' . . . he calls us." "One day he said to me, 'You discovered for yourself what I discovered for the race.'" H.D.
often felt treated as an intellectual equal: "'Of course, you
understand' is the offhand way in which he offers me, from
time to time, some rare discovery, some priceless finding, or
'Perhaps you may feel differently' as if my feelings, my discoveries, were on a par with his own." All this sounds as
though Freud undertook the analysis of H.D. and the others
like her in order to give a group of intellectually special people
a "feel" for psychoanalytic ideas and method.

"The beautiful tone of his voice had a way of taking an
English phrase or sentence out of its context (out of the associated context, you might say, of the whole language)" so that
the word took on special overtones and new life. The analysis
seems to have proceeded much more by this kind of exploration of connotation and association than by ideas about symbols
or theory. "He himself—at least to me personally—deplored
the tendency to *fix* ideas too firmly to set symbols, or to weld

them inexorably," and this caution must have been especially necessary for someone with H.D.'s "myth."

H.D. wrote *Tribute to Freud* almost like a psychoanalysis itself, as a series of free associations, letting her thoughts lead her where they would. The associations are not entirely free, however. She omits so as to protect her privacy, saying almost nothing about her contemporary life and very little about her adult life at all. She is completely silent on matters of adult sexuality (although it is clear that she and Freud worked with infantile sexual material). Instead, she produces a whole series of mythological associations. Most of the time she relies without explanation on connotations and verbal echoes in her own and, particularly, in Freud's phrasings. Only once does she make a straightforward interpretation. We, her readers, are left to make the connections ourselves, though the connections are there to be made, at least for her developmental years.

Because she wrote in a series of free associations, the book became a seamless web: to pick up any one point is to involve oneself in all. Perhaps the best way to give the material sequence is to follow out Freud's changing roles. One would expect H.D. (or any other analysand) in the transference situation of psychoanalysis to transfer or project onto the analyst her positive and negative feelings toward the key figures of her childhood—her mother, her father, and, in H.D.'s case, the brother who was so especially important to her. In seeking, then, the common source in childhood of H.D.'s lifestyle and her literary style, we can use Freud himself, as he is assigned various roles in the transference, for our Ariadne thread.

III

We can enter the labyrinth with H.D., for "Undoubtedly," she noted, "the Professor took an important clue from the first reaction of a new analysand or patient." When first she entered his consulting room, Freud stood waiting for the tall, shy woman of forty-seven to speak. H.D., however, silently took an inventory of the contents of the room, Freud's collection of Greek and Egyptian antiquities. Finally, "waiting and finding that I would not or could not speak, he uttered. What he said—and I thought a little sadly—was, 'You are the only person who has ever come into this room and looked at the things in the room before looking at me.' " The Professor might have taken a clue to H.D.'s tendency to approach someone she desired through an intermediary, particularly a mythological object or symbol.

The first such intermediary in the book is "the Flying Dutchman," J. J. van der Leeuw, so nicknamed because he flew his own plane. "His soul fitted his body," wrote H.D., and she surely had not forgotten that when she wrote, later in the book, of her own soul, "Its body did not fit it very well." When H.D. heard that he had died, she rushed back to Vienna to express her sorrow and sympathy for Freud. " 'You have come,' " he bluntly interpreted, " 'to take his place.' " Indeed, she had said, "We bear the same relation to the couch," and she called van der Leeuw her "brother-in-arms" and "Mercury."

Her brother was in arms when he was killed in France in 1918, and H.D. herself linked soldier and airman when she had her mystical vision at Corfu or when she numbered her brother among the "poised, disciplined and valiant young winged Mercuries" who fell from the air during the war. Freud's remark "that the analysand who preceded me [van der Leeuw] was 'actually considerably taller' " than H.D. led her directly to a statement and a memory, "My brother is considerably taller."

Although she does not even tell us his name, this older brother was obviously a key figure in H.D.'s childhood, for he "is admittedly his mother's favourite." H.D. loved and admired him, too, but she also envied him: "I was not, it was very easy to see, quaint and quick and clever like my brother. My brother? Am I my brother's keeper?" Perhaps she did feel like Cain, for that very brother seemed to be the intermediary through whom she could reach her distant mother: "The trouble is, she knows so many people and they come and interrupt. And besides that, she likes my brother better. If I stay with my brother, become part almost of my brother, perhaps I can get nearer to *her*." They are, she says, mythological twins: "One is sometimes the shadow of the other; often one is lost and the one seeks the other."

What she sought in her brother was her mother, but another memory of him suggests another *motif:* he had taken one of the "sacred objects" from his father's desk, a magnifying glass, and he showed his sister how he could focus the sunlight to burn a piece of paper. Possibly, to become one with her brother meant to acquire the special powers that men seemed to have, the power to bring fire from heaven like Prometheus, to understand the mysterious symbols her astronomer-father used or her brother's larger vocabulary. Thus, her brother was the first of the many mythological lover-heroes in H.D.'s quests: Perseus, Hermes, the Flying Dutchman, the Professors (her father, Freud)—in Norman Holmes Pearson's apt phrase, "the one searched for (who himself searches)." If she became her brother, she would be "quaint and clever" instead of "not very advanced." Perhaps most important, she would have arrived first; she would be older, not a foreigner or " 'a little stranger.' " All these things might be possible with a boy's body instead of a girl's. As she puts it in an enigmatic comment, left to stand by itself after a story about her brother and discoveries under a log, "There were things under things, as well as things inside things."

H.D. suggests still another goal she sought in her brother, another memory, the wish that she could be a mother: perhaps her brother would be her doll's father, perhaps her own father could be. She would be the virgin mother, "building a dream and the dream is symbolized by the . . . doll in her arms." To Freud, in the transference, she brought all these fantasies and investments of her brother, just as she brought the dreams concretized as the doll.

Freud is St. Michael, who will slay the dragon of her fears, but Michael was also regent of the planet Mercury—"in Renaissance paintings, we are not surprised to see Saint Michael wearing the winged sandals and sometimes even the winged helmet of the classic messenger of the Gods." Thus, she has whole chains of associations: "Thoth, Hermes, Mercury, and last, Michael, Captain or Centurion of the hosts of heaven." When she compares Freud to the Centurion of heaven, she cannot have forgotten that ten pages earlier, she had said that, in his refusal to accept her notions of immortality, his slamming the door on visions of the future, he was standing "like the Roman Centurion before the gate of Pompeii, who did not move from his station before the gateway since he had received no orders to do so, and who stood for later generations to wonder at, embalmed in hardened lava, preserved in the very fire and ashes that had destroyed him." She goes on to quote Freud, " 'At least, they have not burnt me at the stake.' " Earlier, she had been grateful that the Professor had not lived until World War II. "He was a handful of ashes" "before the blast and bombing and fires had devastated this city." The wish is kindly meant, but underneath it shows the same ambivalence as toward that other Mercury, her brother.

Freud, like Prometheus, like her brother, had stolen fire from heaven, from the sun, for he was not only the victim but the cause of explosions: "Many of his words did, in a sense, explode . . . opening up mines of hidden treasures." More gently, after an especially striking insight, he would say, " 'Ah —now—we must celebrate *this*' "; he would rise, select, light, and then, "from the niche [where he sat rose] the smoke of burnt incense, the smouldering of his mellow, fragrant cigar."

She identified Freud with Asklepios, the "blameless physician," son of the sun god Apollo. "He was the son of the sun, Phoebos Apollo, and music and medicine were alike sacred to this source of light." "Here was the master-musician, he, too, a son of Apollo, who would harmonize the whole human spirit." She identifies herself as a fellow servant of Apollo, the Priestess or Pythoness of Delphi; thus, she suggests that Freud is her peer and brother. But by punning on "son" and "sun," she makes Apollo himself, the father, the "son."

In short, Freud has come to stand for the whole ambiguous network of wishes and relationships associated with the oedipal wishes of a little girl: that she could become a mother with her brother as father; that she could, by marrying her father, become her brother's mother; that she could, by marrying her brother, become her father's mother. She seems to recognize these ambiguities when she calls Freud "the Old Man of the Sea," Proteus, the shapeshifter, or compares him to two-faced Janus, who leads her to Thoth, Hermes, Mercury, and finally, the Flying Dutchman. But Janus is also Captain January, a beloved old lighthouse keeper who takes in a ship-wrecked child. Freud becomes in the transference not only her brother but also her father. This dual relationship with Freud matches H.D.'s extended identification of herself with Mignon, the boy-girl from *Wilhelm Meister*, who is both sister but also would-be sexual object to the hero, as in the "Piraeus" poem.

Even so, in the strangely labile world of a psychoanalysis, Freud can become H.D.'s father, but so can H.D. She herself makes the connection: her father, being an astronomer, often slept on a couch in his study during the day, and she was not to disturb him. "But now it is I who am lying on the couch in the room lined with books." Her father had in his study a white owl under a bell jar; she has the Professor, sitting "there, quietly, like an old owl in a tree." (And, one should remember, the owl is an emblem for Athené with whom H.D. identified herself.) At the top of the astronomical tables he made up, her father would write something which was neither a letter nor a number: "He will sketch in a hieroglyph; it may stand for one of the Houses or Signs of the Zodiac, or it may be a planet simply: Jupiter or Mars or Venus." Dreams, visions, and all the shapes, lines, and graphs she speaks of are "the hieroglyph of the unconscious." As for herself, "Niké, Victory seemed to be the clue, seemed to be my own special sign or part of my hieroglyph." Similarly, in *Helen in Egypt*, Helen's body becomes the hieroglyph: "She herself is the writing." [17] If one is a writing, one is looked at—by Freud, by the aloof father, perhaps even by the distant mother.

Later H.D. will identify herself with Freud by seeing *him* as victorious, but at the moment we are concerned with Freud's becoming, in the transference, H.D.'s father. For one thing, he seemed able to persist. Her father had died at the shock of learning of her brother's death, while "The Professor had had shock upon shock. But he had not died." Another line of association led to what men have and what doctors do. "My father possessed sacred symbols . . . he, like the Professor, had old, old sacred objects on his study table." In his study, her father had a photograph of Rembrandt's *The Anatomy Lesson*, and her father rather liked to identify himself with doctors. Further, "A doctor has a bag with strange things in it, steel and knives and scissors." Doctors know secrets. Her father "entrusts" her with his paper-knife to cut the pages of some of his journals. "The half-naked man on the table was dead so it did not hurt him when the doctors sliced his arm with a knife or a pair of scissors." She sees psychoanalysis as a special form of Socratic method and Socratic method in turn as fencing. Freud, in the transference, acquired the power to cut and thrust and penetrate. She speaks of the Tree of Knowledge: "His [Freud's] were the great giant roots of that tree, but mine, with hair-like almost invisible feelers . . . the invisible intuitive rootlet . . . the smallest possible sub-soil rootlet," could also solve mysteries.

In his experience, Freud wrote about this time, one of the irreducible difficulties in the analysis of women was the frustration and anger imposed by their strong unconscious wish to recapture a supposedly lost masculine power physically symbolized as the male organ.[18] We should bear in mind this belief (that the analyst—the doctor—will restore what has been, in fantasy, cut off) in considering Freud's interpretive "gifts" to H.D. One day he led her from the couch into his study to show her one of his Greek figurines. " '*This* is my favourite,' he said," and he held out a little bronze Pallas Athené. " 'She is perfect,' he said, '*only she has lost her spear*' " (italics H.D.'s). H.D. remembered that Athené's winged form was Niké, so that this was a Niké without wings, Niké A-pteros, as, for example, H.D. had seen her in Athens (made so that Victory would never fly away to another city). She meditates on "She is perfect." "The little bronze statue was a perfect symbol, made in man's image (in woman's, as it happened), to be venerated as a projection of abstract thought, Pallas Athené . . . sprung full-armed from the head of her father, our-father."

Maybe it wasn't a spear she had been holding—"It might have been a rod or staff," and she went on to remember the occasion when the Professor gave her a little branch from a box of oranges his son had sent. In effect, Freud was giving her symbolically what Freud thought every woman patient wanted. She herself could associate to that golden bough another gift or compliment Freud gave her: "There are very few who understand this [that my discoveries are a basis for a very grave philosophy], *there are very few who are capable of understanding this.*" Freud was, in effect, giving H.D. back the understanding, the brain strength, that leads to victory, the masculine power represented in sacred objects, the ability to live in her wingless self, all of which, at some level of her being, H.D. felt, her real father had taken away. Or, perhaps, her mother had never given her.

From psychoanalytic theory, one would expect the father to inherit the conflicts and feelings associated with the mother. Indeed, H.D. is quite explicit about this: "*If* one could stay near her always, there would be no break in consciousness— but half a loaf is better than no bread and there are things, not altogether negligible, to be said for *him*." Thus, on the occasion when her brother took the magnifying glass, her associations moved from her angry father to a mysterious, beautiful Egyptian princess coming down a flight of steps to find Moses in the bulrushes. "Do I wish myself, in the deepest unconscious or subconscious layers of my being, to be the founder of a new religion?" Religious wishes were her one point of difference with Freud: "About the greater transcendental issues, we never argued. But there was an argument implicit in our very bones," and it was in this context that she cast him as the burnt Centurion.

"We touched lightly on some of the more abstruse transcendental problems, it is true, but we related them to the familiar family-complex." "A Queen or Princess," she notes, "is obvious mother-symbol." Equally obviously, though, her need for a religious level of being does not simply come down to her wish to merge with a "Princess" or "prophetess." Participation in another level of being would make her a mother in a far more powerful sense, for she could then restore her own lost ones. "The dead were living in so far as they lived in memory or were recalled in dream."

Further, the wish for an eternal order might come, not only from the child's wishing to become the mother, but also from the child's wishing to be mothered. The child wishes for a source of love and nurture who is always there—for example, an analyst who never dies or goes away: "I looked at the things in his room before I looked at him; for I knew the things in his room were symbols of Eternity and contained him then, as Eternity contains him now." When Freud one day spoke as though his immortality lay only in his grandchildren, "I felt a sudden gap, a severance, a chasm or schism in consciousness." She was echoing what she had said earlier about her mother: "*If* one could stay near her always, there would be no break in consciousness." Her concern with the Flying Dutchman and Freud's other patients matches her complaint about the many people who "come and interrupt" her relationship with her mother.

In short, H.D. has shown, by making Freud in the transference her mother, how mystical and religious wishes hark back to the early mother-child relationship. The timeless world of myth became, for her, a way of avoiding gaps, breaks, and interruptions between herself and a nurturing other. In later life, Erikson has shown, political ideologies, personal love, or religious faith can all serve the maternal function, gratifying "the simple and fervent wish for a hallucinatory sense of unity with a maternal matrix," [19] and this seems to have been the central function not only of myth and religion for H.D. but also of psychoanalysis itself. It, too, met her need to have faith in something. Thus, Freud interpreted H.D.'s mystical vision on Corfu "as a desire for union with [your] mother," and in the transference he became that mother. " 'Why did you think you had to tell me? . . . . But you wanted to tell your mother.' " Indeed, H.D.'s whole faith in Freud and psychoanalysis should be interpreted as a wish for a mystical union: "The Professor had said in the very beginning that I had come to Vienna hoping to find my mother."

It is not surprising, then, since we are dealing with fantasies of suckling, that H.D. uses images of fluids to describe the psychoanalytic process. She had entered analysis because she felt she was, like other intellectuals, "drifting," that she was "a narrow birch-bark canoe" being swept into the "cataract" of war. Her friends provided only "a deluge of brilliant talk," but no "safe harbour." Thus, she sees herself as "a ship-wrecked child" turning to old Captain January. "The flow of associated images," the "fountain-head of highest truth," "the current [that] ran too deep"—H.D.'s images of fluids suggest, beautifully, the way something which is experienced passively, as an overpowering and terrifying deluge or flood, can, in the microcosm of the analytic relationship, be accepted and mastered. "He would stand guardian, he would turn the whole stream of consciousness back into useful, into *irrigation* channels."

Other images of fluids show the feeling of "oceanic" unity that is related to that first unity with the mother. She describes Freud as naming and discovering "a great stream or ocean underground" that, "overflowing," produces inspiration, madness, or creative idea. This ocean transcends all barriers of time and space. Thus, for any patient, "his particular stream, his personal life, could run clear of obstruction into the great river of humanity, hence to the sea of superhuman perfection." H.D. had indeed "come to Vienna hoping to find her mother," even as she had found her on Corfu.

IV

In her vision, she began to see pictures outlined in light on the wall of the hotel room she shared with Bryher. The first was a head-and-shoulders silhouette of a soldier or airman with a visored cap. The second "was the conventional outline of a goblet or cup, actually suggesting the mystic chalice, but it was the familiar goblet shape we all know, with round base and glass-stem." The third is another mythological adaptation of a familiar object: the stand for a small spirit-lamp metamorphosed into the tripod on which the prophetess at Delphi sat. H.D. sees the tripod as the triad of religion, art, and medicine. These figures—hieroglyphs she calls them—appear like formal patterns stamped on playing-cards. As in many of H.D.'s psychic patterns, however, she cannot tell whether she is projecting the images or whether "they are projected from outside."

Around the base of the tripod appears a swarm of tiny people, like insects. "They were people, they were annoying." H.D. seemed to accept Freud's interpretation of the vision "as a suppressed desire for forbidden 'signs and wonders,' breaking bounds, a suppressed desire to be a Prophetess, to be important anyway, megalomania they call it." And perhaps this megalomanic fantasy is why the people appeared as a swarm of "small midges." At any rate, the people disappear, and the pictures begin to move upward.

Two dots of light appear and trace lines toward each other until they meet and become one line. H.D. is stiff, she says, as though she were looking at the Gorgon head. The dots form another line, then another, then a series. H.D. feels as though she is drowning. "I must be born again or break utterly." The lines become a Jacob's ladder linking heaven and earth.

The last figure forms: "There she is, I call her she; I call her Niké, Victory," around her a pattern of half-S's—question marks. "She is a common-or-garden angel," three-dimensional, floating up the ladder, "free and with wings." "Niké, Victory seemed to be the clue, seemed to be my own especial sign or part of my hieroglyph." "I thought, 'Helios, the sun . . .' And I shut off, 'cut out' before the final picture, before (you might say) the explosion took place." H.D. let go, then, from complete exhaustion, but, in this strange, mystical experience, Bryher "who has been waiting by me, carries on 'the reading' where I left off." Until H.D. dropped her head in her hands, Bryher saw nothing, but then she saw "the last concluding symbol." "She said, it was a circle like the sun-disc and a figure within the disc; a man, she thought, was reaching out to draw the image of a woman (my Niké?) into the sun beside him."

Obviously, this vision has an almost unbelievable richness of symbol, association, and theme. It consolidated a whole mass of charged materials for H.D. No wonder she felt completely exhausted; no wonder Freud singled out this vision "as the most dangerous or the only actually dangerous 'symptom.'" Indeed, she originally entitled the memoir "Writing on the Wall," but went along with Norman Holmes Pearson's suggestion of a change.

As one would expect, the final vision is the least defended against or disguised, the first vision the most so. To the last picture, H.D. associates memories of her father and mother, and to be the chosen woman of the man in the sun-disc would indeed involve an "explosion." H.D. herself, however, suggests another interpretation and association: "The shrine of Helios (Hellas, Helen) had been really the main objective of my journey." "I was physically in Greece, in Hellas (Helen). I had come home to the glory that was Greece," and she identifies the phrase as from "Edgar Allan Poe's much-quoted *Helen*, and my mother's name was Helen."

Such associations take us back to early, hungry wishes for a timeless at-oneness with the mother. Now H.D. is victorious in her quest. There is, however, still another pattern of fusion: the vision is not only H.D.'s; it is also Bryher's, a further blurring of the boundaries between self and nurturing other. Discrete dots appear but merge to form a Jacob's ladder linking earth to the realm of the gods, like a child's wish to merge into the world of the parents.

To this paragraph, however, H.D. associated staring at the Gorgon's head, thus identifying herself both with Athené's enemies (turned to stone by Perseus' weapon) and with Perseus himself, "guided by Athené (or was it Hermes, Mercury?)." The Gorgon head is both "an enemy to be dealt with," "the ugly Head or Source of evil," but also, "He was himself to manipulate his weapon, this ugly severed head of the enemy of Wisdom and Beauty." She seems to be saying the vision—the sight itself—combines a man's weapon with female hostility, much as, in one of her poems, she describes lovemaking as two weapons one of which will "break" "my own lesser," "tempered in different heat." [20] There are few symbols with universal unconscious meaning, and Freud was quite right to caution H.D. against one-to-one symbolic decodings. But her wordings and her juxtaposition of male power with an ugly, evil, ignorant source—cut off—matches exactly the classical psychoanalytic interpretation of the Gorgon's head and its power to rigidify. It symbolizes the child's sight of the contrast between male genitals as a presence and the female as an absence, together with the fear or disgust he may feel and the frantic defenses he may interpose against the possibility of the one transforming into the other.[21] Here, however, H.D. gives the image her distinctive style: she uses it to bring together both positive and negative aspects of both male and female, parents and child, physical and abstract, as she does in the other hollow parts of her vision.

Still working backwards through H.D.'s images, we come to the tripod, a homely, familiar object. It is the "base" for the spirit-lamp, but it is also what the Pythoness of Delphi sat on. It may also represent a feminine concern with inner or enclosed spaces. Certainly her description of it stresses the emptiness of its circles. Yet it is this stand that is associated with megalomania—again, we seem to be coming to the theme of overcompensating for what she feels is another gap, that in her feminine body. What the prophetess sits on is at once "homely" but "all the more an object to be venerated."

The "soldier or airman" H.D. herself identifies as "dead brother? lost friend?" In any case, he seems to represent that hard, weaponed masculinity that H.D. longed to fuse with. Between this masculine figure and the tripod is the chalice, another "familiar" object transformed. H.D. associates it with the "mystic chalice," hence with a quest of some kind. Like the tripod, it is empty, and its place in the sequence suggests a relation between earliest hunger and the quest for a lost masculinity or masculine figure.

V

To sum up, in the mystical vision H.D. does two things: she concretizes the abstract; she mythologizes the commonplace. The vision on Corfu brings us to the heart of the H.D.-myth. It was implicit in her first meeting Freud's things, then Freud: to approach the outer object of an inner desire through an intermediary. We can now explicate those terms. The intermediary is perfect, timeless, symbolic (that is, mythological, hieroglyphic); filled, it combines past and future, male and female, with "no interruptions." The outer object tends to be hard, real, everyday, prosaic, even brutal, while the inner desire is vague, soft, empty, abstract, and spiritual. We can make at least a preliminary statement of the H.D.-myth: *When I concretize the spiritual or mythologize the everyday, I create a perfect, timeless hieroglyph-world which I can be and be in.* Or, *I want to close the gap with signs.* Moreover, in her poems and her writing about her analysis, H.D. shows how she (or any human being) transforms such a myth through all the modalities associated with the developmental zones of childhood and into all the recurring issues of her life as a woman and as a poet.

Consider, in the H.D.-myth, the theme of fusion with a timeless, uninterrupted region of immortality (related originally, I would think, to H.D.'s childhood wishes toward her mother, although she often imaged it as a union of male and female, like Helios-Helen in the sun-disc). For example, H.D. repeatedly insists that the core of Freud's achievement was a fusion: "He had brought the past into the present with his *the childhood of the individual is the childhood of the race*—or is it the other way round?—*the childhood of the race is the childhood of the individual.*" H.D. could see her living in England as an attempt at fusion:

The sea grows narrower, the gap in consciousness sometimes seems negligible; nevertheless there is a duality, the English-speaking peoples are related, brothers, twins even, but they are not one. So in me, 2 distinct racial or biological or psychological entities tend to grow nearer or to blend, even, as time heals old breaks in consciousness.

The blending of the two nationalities in her ancestry resembles the dots merging in the vision or her comment on Shakespeare's possible homosexuality: "Pied? Dappled, two-colored, part-coloured, two-souled. Where was the advantage in that, *O master-mistress of my passion?*" [22] The concern with gaps and breaks in consciousness remind one not only of her thoughts about her bodily gap but the deeper wish, "If one could stay near her always, there would be no break in consciousness." Thus her quest for timelessness and immortality stems from a deeper wish to avoid the interruptions she perceived as marring her earliest relation with her mother.

"If I stay with my brother, become part almost of my brother, perhaps I can get nearer to *her*." Fusion with a man meant both fusion with and escape from the mother:

> Hermes, Hermes
> the great sea foamed,
> gnashed its teeth about me;
> but you have waited,
> where sea-grass tangles with
> shore-grass.[23]

To join Hermes—whom other poems identify with writing and insight—is to escape from a chaos that threatens to engulf you. You find him at the boundary between the sea-mouth and the security of land, where things are tactile and hairlike, no longer foam.

The figure of André in her charming children's book, *The Hedgehog*,[24] suggests the kind of firm knowledge or bristly possessions one might get from a brother. The story works out H.D.'s recurring pattern: replacing something needed and missing by a magical word (the meaning of which this little heroine does not know). What is an *hérisson?* "Little girls shouldn't ask," but André has one. Why should she ask the moon for things André can get? The *hérisson* is something someone gives you, "big as a mountain," associated with the fur of her mother's coat, with having babies, and with frightening snakes away. Although the book was written in 1925, the figure of Dr. Berne Blum, who reassures the heroine about these matters, markedly foreshadows Freud, further evidence that H.D. had such a strong positive transference in 1933 because Freud fitted into a matrix of pre-existing fantasies and expectations toward fatherly doctors, professors, and men in general.

Fusion with a man could stave off deficiency: thus H.D. found it easy to project into and identify with Freud. But fusion with a man also makes the man into a mother, and H.D. associated the Berggasse, Freud's street, with Athens, which she had already associated to her mother and her childhood home. In still a third variant, fusion with a male meant that H.D. could assume the mother-role herself, as when she wished to give, like Alcestis, her own life to Freud, or, in her last words about Freud: "O, let's go away together, pleads the soul," then retreating to "the simple affirmation . . . of uttermost veneration." Like any classicist, she knew the etymology of that word and built on it one of her most moving poems to the Great Mother:

> Swiftly re-light the flame,
> Aphrodite, holy name,

Astarte, hull and spar
of wrecked ships lost your star,

forgot the light at dusk,
forgot the prayer at dawn;

return, O holiest one,
Venus whose name is kin

to venerate,
venerator.[25]

(1945)

Yet, within such reverend love, there is a core of coldness that
shows in another of H.D.'s best poems, used as the dedication
of *Palimpsest* to Bryher, although her father was the astronomer, and her mother (to judge from the poem you have just
read) the real "North Star."

Stars wheel in purple, yours is not so rare
as Hesperus, nor yet so great a star
as bright Aldeberan or Sirius,
nor yet the stained and brilliant one of War;

stars turn in purple, glorious to the sight;
yours is not gracious as the Pleiads are
nor as Orion's sapphires, luminous;

yet disenchanted, cold, imperious face,
when all the others blighted, reel and fall,
your star, steel-set, keeps lone and frigid tryst
to freighted ships, baffled in wind and blast.

(1925)

Other poems reveal anger and bitterness behind such veneration, and their roots in the first love-hate for the mother. This
painful poem, for example, drew on the feminine and masculine Hebrew words for "bitter":

Now polish the crucible
and in the bowl distill

a word most bitter, *marah,*
a word bitterer still, *mar,*

sea, brine, breaker, seducer,
giver of life, giver of tears;

now polish the crucible
and set the jet of flame

Under, till *marah-mar*
are melted, fuse and join

and change and alter,
mer, mere, mère, mater, Maia, Mary,

Star of the Sea,
Mother.[26]

The astronomer-father, that distant mother, the deserting
lover, here equated in the two forms of the oral word "bitter"
—how H.D. must have longed for closeness, yet feared it as
destruction!

The opposite of closeness in the H.D.-myth is the sense
of being isolated, left out, a foreigner who exists, as it were,
in the third person. "It was a girl between two boys; but,
ironically, it was wispy and mousey, while the boys were glow-
ing and gold." As she says in "Adonis,"

each of us like you
stands apart, like you
fit to be worshipped.
(1917)

She is painful on the subject of the two's in her family—"There
were 2 of everybody (except myself)." In her memories in
Tribute to Freud (mother with brother on the curbstone;

father with brother and the magnifying-glass), in her dreams (the Princess and the baby), or in her visions (the serpent and the thistle; Helios and the Niké-angel), H.D. finds herself in triangular situations, watching the other two—the triumphant climax of the Corfu vision is to end this isolation and fuse with Helios and Bryher. Similarly, she lives an exile in England or Switzerland as though acting out over and over again her own separateness. By coming for her analytic hour on a day when rifles were stacked on the street corners and no other patients appeared, she acted out once again her sense of her difference: "*I am here because no one else has come.* As if again, symbolically, I must be different."

To compromise between being totally included and totally excluded, H.D. liked to take the active role and establish the boundaries and edges of things herself. For example, she gives a highly detailed cartography of Freud's consulting room and study, wall by wall and door by door. Her vision came in units or steps like the cards in fortune-telling, and she could even see her dreams and visions as "steps in the . . . mechanism of supernormal, abnormal (or subnormal) states of mind." The word "steps" itself reminds her of the steps the Princess was descending or the Jacob's ladder in the Corfu vision.

This over-concern for boundaries and discrete units relates to H.D.'s choppy stanza forms, her difficulties with the boundaries of sentences, or the indeterminacy of the verb forms in the Aphrodite-Astarte lyric. Certainly it has something to do with her insistence on treating symbols as having fixed meanings and the dream as "a universal language," despite Freud's cautions to the contrary. I suspect that this was the point at which the analysis could go no further: the wish or need to convert the insubstantial into something both substantial and immortal. This had become too basic a defensive strategy in H.D.'s character to be changed in a few months; this "was an argument implicit in our very bones." This one de-

fense or adaptation met both sides of the H.D.-myth: the wish
to fuse with something (father, brother, mother); the related
wish to close the gap and restore what was missing (inter-
rupted mother, dead brother, dead father, lost masculinity,
missing penis); the defense of meeting only on the basis of a
bounded and defined sign.

The analysis itself was, for her, a search for a missing object and an attempt almost concretely to remake it. "We had
come together in order to substantiate something. I did not
know what." She thought of Freud as a Jewish dealer in antiquities: "This pound of flesh was a *pound of spirit* between
us, something tangible, to be weighed and measured, to be
weighed in the balance and—pray God—not to be found wanting!" In the analysis, she felt, "Thoughts were things, to be
collected, collated, analysed, shelved or resolved. Fragmentary
ideas . . . were sometimes skilfully pieced together" like the
jars and bowls and vases Freud's office displayed. Her special
"memories, visions, dreams, reveries . . . are real. They are as
real in their dimension of length, breadth, thickness, as any of
the bronze or marble or pottery or clay objects that fill the
cases around the walls." Such a wish for a rigid reality carries
inevitably with it a fear: "There are dreams or sequences of
dreams that follow a line . . . like a crack on a bowl that
shows the bowl or vase may at any moment fall in pieces."

H.D. makes a more familiar analogy to unconscious materials: Freud unlocks "vaults and caves" in his "unearthing
buried treasures." His findings can include "priceless treasures,
gems and jewels" or junk: "What he offered as treasure, this
revelation that he seemed to value, was poor stuff, trash indeed,
ideas that a ragpicker would pass over in disdain." The first
object from below was the child's own body products,
precious in some contexts, trash in others.[27]

In general, H.D. looks askance at products which are soft
like rags. When, for example, Freud refers to an insight as

"striking oil," H.D. hardens his discovery into finding "the carved symbol of an idea or a deathless dream" or stresses "the outer rock or shale, the accumulation of hundreds or thousands of years." Oil itself she makes a "concrete definite image." " 'I struck oil' suggests business enterprise. We visualize stark uprights and skeleton-like steel cages, like unfinished Eiffel Towers." Then, having concretized or phallicized the oil, H.D. attributes to others the fantasy that psychoanalysis is a system for getting something precious out of you, "some mechanical construction set up in an arid desert, to trap the unwary, and if there is 'oil' to be inferred, the 'oil' goes to someone else; there are astute doctors who 'squeeze you dry' with their exorbitant fees for prolonged and expensive treatments."

Down in that cloacal region where the Professor has "tunnelled" are "the chasms or gulfs where the ancient dragon lives." On the one hand, Freud is the St. Michael or Hercules who will slay "the Dragon . . . the Hydra-headed monster." On the other hand, H.D. herself had "come to a strange city, to beard him, himself, the dragon, in his very den? Vienna? Venice? My mother had come here on her honeymoon. . . ." H.D. admits the analysis ended before she dealt with her own war fears, "my own personal little Dragon of war-terror." Nevertheless, she ordered him "back to his subterranean cavern."

There he growled and bit on his chains and was only loosed finally, when the full apocryphal terror of fire and brimstone, of whirlwind and flood and tempest, of the Biblical Day of Judgement and the Last Trump, became no longer abstractions, terrors too dreadful to be thought of, but things that were happening every day, every night, and at one time, at every hour of the day and night, to myself and my friends.

In this (to use the clinical term) "world destruction fantasy," we get a glimpse of that overpowering rage and fear someplace in H.D.'s development, associated with fire and flood as destroyers, with the subterranean caves of her body, with terrors in the night, with the abstract and inner becoming concrete, and, I would guess, most deeply with the resentment the little girl must have felt toward the mother who rejected her and preferred her brother.

Clearly, all these feelings were brought up again by the two wars. Equally clearly, H.D. did not finally deal with them in the analysis. Yet it is well to remember that she did her most distinguished creative work during those two wars: a graphic illustration of the theory that artistic creativity stems from the wish to reconstitute what has been lost in aggressive fantasy. Consider this excerpt from a poem she wrote about the same time as *Tribute to Freud:*

> Hermes Trismegistus
>
> spears, with Saint Michael,
> the darkness of ignorance,
>
> casts the Old Dragon
> into the abyss.[28]

In *Tribute*, she identified Freud both with the dragon and with Michael-Hermes-Thoth who in turn stood for the writer— H.D. herself. Both *Tribute* and the poem unite H.D. with dragon and dragon-killer, with both sides of those she ambivalently loved.

A dragon breathes destructive fire. A dragon also has wings, and we have already seen how wings were associated in H.D.'s mind with the phallic powers of a Flying Dutchman, Mercury, Niké, her brother, or, generally, with "the black wing of man's growing power of destruction." It is not just whimsy to say that one of Freud's great achievements in the analysis was to get his patient to accept herself as wingless. Wings, she learned, symbolized flight, not power, really, but just the opposite: "Perhaps my trip to Greece, that spring, might have

been interpreted as a flight from reality. Perhaps my experiences there [among them, the vision] might be translated as
another flight—from a flight." "We must forgo a flight from
reality." The Flying Dutchman "flew too high and flew too
quickly," an idiom she applied to her own quest for an absolute. Flying killed van der Leeuw, and Freud singled out
H.D.'s "writing-on-the-wall" as the most dangerous symptom,
"a suppressed desire for . . . breaking bounds . . . megalomania," in which people appeared as midges—as they would
from an airplane.

Quite the opposite of these unbounded flights was the
adaptive, more discrete way H.D. saw her life, in terms of
Holmes's "Chambered Nautilus." The shell was linked in her
mind to her preoccupation with immortality, "the personal
soul's existence in some form or other, after it has shed the
outworn or outgrown body." "Build thee more stately mansions, O my soul," and she felt she had, in coming to the
Professor. Her work with him seemed to "justify all the spiral-
like meanderings of my mind and body. I had come home, in
fact." She could speak of her "curled involuted or convoluted
shell skull, and inside the skull, the curled, intricate hermit-like
mollusc, the brain-matter itself." She developed the image in
one of her most admired lyrics, written about the same time
as *Tribute to Freud:*

> There is a spell, for instance
> in every sea-shell:
>
> continuous, the seathrust
> is powerless against coral,
>
> bone, stone, marble
> hewn from within by that craftsman,
>
> the shell-fish:
> oyster, clam, mollusc

is master-mason planning
the stone marvel:

yet that flabby, amorphous hermit
within, like the planet

senses the finite,
it limits its orbit

of being, its house,
temple, fane, shrine:

it unlocks the portals
at stated intervals:

Prompted by hunger,
it opens to the tide-flow:

but infinity? no,
of nothing-too-much

I sense my own limit,
my shell-jaws snap shut

at invasion of the limitless,
ocean-weight; infinite water

can not crack me, egg in egg-shell;
closed in, complete, immortal

full-circle, I know the pull
of the tide, the lull

as well as the moon;
the octopus-darkness

is powerless against
her cold immortality;

so I in my own way know
that the whale

can not digest me:
be firm in your own small, static, limited

orbit and the shark-jaws
of outer circumstance

will spit you forth:
be indigestible, hard, ungiving,

so that, living within,
you beget, self-out-of-self,

selfless,
that pearl-of-great-price.[29]

(1942)

The poem sums up many of H.D.'s thoughts about herself: her need for a hard protective boundary; within it, the self, felt as soft and vulnerable; within that self, the equally precious work of art, but hard, and so symbolizing and creating (as the "pearl of great price" did) the Kingdom of Heaven.

The work of art had to be made hard, to show that "Thoughts are things," and it was for such a hardness she longed, even of sounds and smells as in the early poem, "Sheltered Garden":

O for some sharp swish of a branch—
there is no scent of resin
in this place,
no taste of bark, of coarse weeds,
aromatic, astringent—
only border on border of scented pinks.

(1916)

Imagism by its very directness served her need to be crisply separate.

Softness, by contrast, implied fusion, as in her extended image of Freud unraveling the threads of her unconscious mind or her statement: "The shuttle of the years ran a thread that wove my pattern into the Professor's." She "painfully unravelled a dingy, carelessly woven strip of tapestry," something sordid in her life. When Freud spoke, however, it was

as if he had dipped the grey web of conventionally woven thought and with it, conventionally *spoken* thought, into a vat of his own brewing—or held a strip of that thought, ripped from the monotonous faded and outworn texture of the language itself, into the bubbling cauldron of his own mind in order to draw it forth dyed blue or scarlet, a new colour to the old grey mesh, a scrap of thought, even a cast-off rag, that would become hereafter a pennant, a standard, a *sign* again, to indicate a direction or, fluttering aloft on a pole, to lead an army.

H.D. needed to turn something soft like cloth into something brightly colored, thrust phallically in the air, emblem of military hardness and force.

By contrast, "We all know that almost invisible thread-line on the cherished glass butter-dish that predicts it will 'come apart in me 'ands' sooner or later—sooner, more likely." Breaking is her image for dying in "Adonis," while birth is becoming hard:

> Each of us like you
> has died once,
> each of us like you
> has passed through drift of wood-leaves,
> cracked and bent
> and tortured and unbent
> in the winter frost,
> then burnt into gold points,
> lighted afresh,
> crisp amber, scales of gold-leaf,
> gold turned and re-welded
> in the sun-heat.

> (1917)

It would be easy to see H.D.'s longing to create, then fuse with hard objects as purely defensive or pathological: the attempt to re-create a lost masculinity or a "hard" ungiving mother. But it is perfectly clear that this symptom or character trait had adaptive virtues as well. To it, we owe H.D.'s interest in and ability to bring out her unconscious life in enduring artistic forms, which she knew would transcend the cataclysms of war:

> But we fight for life,
> we fight, they say, for breath,
>
> so what good are your scribblings?
> this—we take them with us
>
> beyond death; Mercury, Hermes, Thoth
> invented the script, letters, palette;
>
> the indicated flute or lyre-notes
> on papyrus or parchment
>
> are magic, indelibly stamped
> on the atmosphere somewhere,
>
> forever; remember, O Sword,
> you are the younger brother, the latter-born
>
> your Triumph, however exultant,
> must one day be over,
>
> *in the beginning*
> *was the Word.*[30]

(1944)

In her Corfu vision, she paused between images "as if a painter had stepped back from a canvas the better to regard the composition of the picture, or a musician had paused at the music-stand." "This writing-on-the-wall is merely an extension of the artist's mind, a *picture* or an illustrated poem."

To create a work of art was to immortalize an inner wish,

to create as well immortal persons ministering to immortal selves.

> we are the keepers of the secret,
> the carriers, the spinners
>
> of the rare intangible thread
> that binds all humanity
>
> to ancient wisdom,
> to antiquity;
>
> our joy is unique, to us,
> grape, knife, cup, wheat
>
> are symbols in eternity,
> and every concrete object
>
> has abstract value, is timeless
> in the dream parallel
>
> whose relative sigil has not changed
> since Nineveh and Babel.[31]
>
> (1944)

Sigil, signet, *signum*—she talks about these words in *Tribute to Freud*. "And as I write that last word, there flashes into my mind the associated *in hoc signum* or, rather, it must be *in hoc signo* and *vinces*." (I am reminded of the "megalomania" Freud found in the "dangerous symptom" of the Corfu vision.) "Signet," too, had its associations, among them, "the royal signature, usually only the initials of the sovereign's name. (I have used my initials H.D. consistently as my writing signet or sign-manual, though it is only, at this very moment . . . that I realize that my writing signature has anything remotely suggesting sovereignty or the royal manner.)"

VI

She did indeed close up the gap with signs and, in doing so, left behind her a body of poems we honor her for. She also left behind this unique document, *Tribute to Freud*, from which we have been able to infer an "H.D.-myth" as it evolved through the successive psychosexual stages of her own development and as it revealed itself through Freud's taking on a succession of roles in the transference: brother, father, oedipal mother, and, most important, the cosmic, nurturing mother of earliest infancy. I would state that "myth" as exactly (and therefore as ambiguously) as I can: *to close up the gap between inner and outer, spiritual and physical, male and female, by perfect, timeless signs which she can be and be in.* But what does such a "myth" mean? What *is* it? Except for Yeats's "fancy" that such a myth would "make us understand" all someone did or thought, we have no theoretical place to put it.

To place such a "myth" involves us in an excursion into psychoanalytic theory—specifically, into that essay which, if I had to choose, I would select as the single most important contribution to psychoanalysis by someone other than Freud: Robert Waelder's classic, "The Principle of Multiple Function" (1930). As Fenichel summarizes it,

Under the name of "the principle of multiple function" Waelder has described a phenomenon of cardinal importance in ego psychology. This principle expresses the tendency of the organism toward inertia, that is, the tendency to achieve a maximum of effect with a minimum of effort. Among various possible actions that one is chosen which best lends itself to the simultaneous satisfaction of demands from several sources. An action fulfilling a demand of the external world may at the same time result in instinctual gratification and in satisfying the superego.[32]

More exactly, Waelder sees the ego as mediating among four structures or functions that act on it: id and superego, reality and the repetition compulsion. These four forces acting on the ego show a neat symmetry. The id pushes for the expression of sexual and aggressive drives; the superego tries to inhibit them. The repetition compulsion tends to keep the ego doing what it did before, while reality (because it constantly changes) constantly demands new solutions from the ego. These four forces press on the ego, and in that sense the ego passively mediates among them. But the ego also assigns itself the task of testing and probing the four forces, and in this sense the ego actively seeks out problems and solutions. *Every psychic act results from the ego's actively and passively seeking an optimum balance of the forces impinging on it.*

One could draw a simple analogy to driving a car. The driver has an id-like press to get where he is going, perhaps too a pleasure in high speeds and passing other drivers. But he also has superego fears of the highway police or the driver behind him, also guilt and anxiety, perhaps, about accidents. In a short-term way, the inertia of the car keeps him going the way he was going (like the repetition compulsion); in a longer span, his habits of driving and the turns and twists he is used to making on this route do the same. But reality, in the form of changed weather or traffic, may demand new solutions. In this sense, these large forces impinge on the driver to create large feelings of pleasure or danger. But he may also test these forces out actively, creating for himself and responding to smaller signals of danger or pleasure. He may test his braking on a slippery road or drive up close enough to see that it wasn't really a police car after all. He may check the time of an old route against a new one or try the exhilaration of a higher speed, perhaps finding that then the car feels nervously unstable.

Waelder points out, in the manner of Hegel or Marx, that once the ego has adopted a solution, that very act changes the circumstances and begins to make the solution inadequate.

Deciding on a vocation, for example, solves some conflicts but leads to new reality problems—new skills to be learned, new people met, and so on, just as driving one mile brings you to the problems and decisions of the next.

Waelder's essay shows, then, how every psychic act is over-determined. Any ego choice represents a new compromise among eight groups of problems, the ego's active and passive relations with the four forces to which it must respond. He thus considerably simplifies the concept of neurosis. If we regard neurosis as a conflict between two or three psychic agencies, then there are eighty-four possible types of neurosis, and the word ceases to have much use or meaning—one does better simply to specify the type of conflict. Certainly, "multiple function" shows why the various attempts to look at artistic creativity as a function of "neurosis" have been clumsy and misinforming.

Instead, Waelder's essay makes it possible to see the connections between creativity and the rest of a life. As early as 1908, for example, Freud observed:

The sexual behaviour of a human being often *lays down the pattern* for all his other modes of reacting to life. If a man is energetic in winning the object of his love, we are confident that he will pursue his other aims with an equally unswerving energy; but if, for all sorts of reasons, he refrains from satisfying his strong sexual instincts his behaviour will be conciliatory and resigned rather than vigorous in other spheres of life as well.[33]

The concept of rationalization suggests how ideas that pretend to be purely intellectual may serve instinctual or defensive strategies, and by 1945 Abram Kardiner had shown how all ideologies and value systems reflected a mixture of conscious and unconscious needs.[34] Heinz Hartmann demonstrated that a person's moral behavior (his superego style) would reflect his personality just as much as his instinctual life. Other writers have shown how prose style matches the total personality, and

Anna Freud, in 1966, could speak of "a general cognitive and
perceptive style of the ego" which described not only the ego's
dealing with drives or anxiety but "also its everyday functioning such as perceiving, thinking, abstracting, conceptualizing."
Such a style would "embrace the area of conflict as well as
the conflict-free area of secondary process functioning." [35]
Waelder himself and, following him, Roy Schafer showed how
"the principle of multiple function" implied that any given defense must also satisfy the drives it is defending against. [36]

In effect, all these clinicians and theorists are saying the
same simple thing: there is *one* style that operates in *all* the
ego's activities, in all its mediations among the four forces it
must respond to and even—if there can be such a thing—in
any "autonomous" or "conflict-free" sphere. [37] And, indeed,
how could a "style" be otherwise? Does not the very concept
of an organism require that all its parts obey the same principles? As Fenichel summed the matter up, "The mode of rec-
onciling various tasks to one another is characteristic for a
given personality. Thus the ego's habitual modes of adjustment
to the external world, the id, and the superego, and the characteristic types of combining these modes with one another
constitute character." [38] Or you could call it a personal style
or (following Yeats) a "myth" or (to adapt an Adlerian term)
"lifestyle."

What any such phrasing does is establish an idea of organic
unity, which literary people have as much experience of as
psychoanalysts, and perhaps more. For example, an existential
therapist speaks of someone not "getting" a poem:

He fails in his attempts at a conception of the poem which will
"work" by tying together all the elements. Now a friend . . .
suggests to him an over-all organization or unifying meaning-
scheme which had not occurred to him. Suddenly it "clicks."

The words, without some unifying scheme of meanings, are
not a poem. A poem is an experience which is generated only as

there is also brought to bear some unifying scheme by the one who interprets.

Now I propose that the patient in insight therapy plays a role analogous to that of the reader of the poem: what the patient "reads" are the bits and pieces of his life. He brings these fragments of his life to the therapist who then suggests a meaning-scheme in terms of which to reorganize and unify the patient's experience.[39]

While that analogy overintellectualizes analytic insight, Freud himself, most direct of therapists, generalized from the Wolf-Man about the unity implied by a psychoanalytic explanation, "how, after a certain phase of the treatment, everything seemed to converge upon it, and how later, in the synthesis, the most various and remarkable results radiated out from it; how not only the large problems but the smallest peculiarities in the history of the case were cleared up by this single assumption." [40]

Among today's psychoanalysts, the one who has best grasped the organic unity in the psyche is Heinz Lichtenstein, with his concept of an "identity theme." A person comes into the world with a certain rather general style or "temperament" or "initial organizing configuration." A baby will be "easy" or "difficult" or "slow to warm up" according to whether he is more or less intense, regular, responsive, distractable, or adaptable.[41] Such general traits admit of a great range of behavior. Some will suit a mother and some will not, but out of the "fit" of mother and baby, be it good or bad, the child's personality will develop. "The specific unconscious need of the mother . . . actualizes out of these infinite potentialities one way of being in the child, namely being the child for this particular mother, responding to her unique and individual needs." This way of being Lichenstein calls a "primary identity," "a zero point which must precede all other mental developments."

We then develop further in rhythmic oscillations: first the self and then the people around us maintain our identity. This continuing rhythm leads to "the concept of a primary identity as an invariant the transformations of which we could call development," much like a musical theme and variations. Within this pattern, mental developments become "possible" or "impossible" depending on inner and outer reality. First, are they possible transformations of the invariant identity theme? Second, can one translate the "organizing directions" given by that primary identity into inner and outer actuality? [42]

The "identity theme" itself cannot change, however, as Lichtenstein shows with his classic case, Anna S., whose theme could be "transcribed by the concept of being another one's 'essence.' " Therapy could change Anna's prostitution and Lesbianism to real love for a man, but in that relationship too she could say, "Does real loving make one feel a part of another? When he makes love to me I really feel that I'm way down deep inside of him, that his arms are my arms, etc." [43] Even in child therapy, concludes Erik Erikson, "Therapy and guidance may attempt to substitute more desirable identifications for undesirable ones, but the total configuration of the ego identity remains unalterable." [44]

From the point of view of an observer, "The *perception* of the 'whole person' means the process of abstracting an invariant from the multitude of transformations. This invariant, when perceived in our encounter with another individual, we describe as the individual's personality," says Lichtenstein.[45] Or "character" or "style" or "identity theme." We could have derived H.D.'s personal myth from the invariances in her poems and fictions, but because she left us something more—the memoir of her analysis—she enables us to take one step further toward understanding creativity and the maker's mind.

VII

To close the gap with signs—this is H.D.'s "myth" or "ego identity" or character or "identity theme," the style with which her ego mediates among the forces acting on it. We have seen it pervade all her writing and all that we know of her adult life. Yet, Lichtenstein reminds us, such an adult life style develops through the psychosexual sequence of development, permeating at every stage "all [she] did and thought." And we can see this development only because H.D. has left us, in *Tribute to Freud*, her reconstruction with Freud of the lost kingdoms of infancy.

As for so many lyric poets, the psychosexual mode that dominated H.D.'s psyche is the earliest: that stage when life simply *was* the oral relationship between nurturing mother and feeding child. As we see her in the analysis, at her very center, H.D. wished and feared to fuse with, be devoured by, close the gap between herself and a mother perceived and felt as a timeless, uninterrupted, unbroken mystic level of experience. She wished for the nurturer and feared the withholder, and the adult memories show that the infant dealt with this mingling of wish and fear, love and hate, by transforming inner and outer reality. She transformed the everyday imperfections and frustrations of the outer world into a more perfect and permanent mythology. She concretized her inchoate, inner longings into hard, tangible, reachable realities—again, usually, mythological. In classical myth and other poetic signs, both the child and the adult found a compromise: perfections she could have. Then, as an adult, she became the poet of hard, cold classicism or, alternatively, bristly pine trees and hedgehogs. The strategy was a cosmic one and gave rise to her imagery of oceans and floods crashing and breaking and her destructive fantasies of a fiery world destruction. To close the gap with signs is to be nurtured by a myth.

The first psychosexual stage colors its successors, although some of those later stages involved H.D. more than others. Her writings and her analysis show little concern with the next, however, that which focuses on the retention and elimination of body products and the achievement of autonomy (as against shame and doubt) in the child's relations with adults who try to control this special mode of communication. We have seen how H.D. wished to transform soft, dirty, oily, rag-like, or heated objects into cold, hard, firm works of art. Soft materials, as she describes them in the analysis, might be forced out of her by another, might belong to that other (a later form of the earlier fear about fusion), while hard objects would be her own creation and the definite signs the child had already made central to her ego style.

The awe accorded her father and the strength and clever-ness of her older brothers (some from her father's first mar-riage and quite a bit older) gave the next psychosexual devel-opment special importance for H.D. At this stage, the child begins to try to be like its parents, to move, talk, know, make—in general, to intrude upon the world. Yet along with these ambitions comes a sense of inadequacy in that the parents, being bigger, seem always to be better as well. For the little girl, this sense of inadequacy is heightened by her knowledge of the one respect in which a little boy is bigger (and therefore perceived as better or more like an adult) than she.

To judge from H.D.'s remarks in the analysis and her poetic preoccupation with hard, pointed things, the little girl's already over-determined wish to create a hard object must have taken on a new function in this stage: replacing the missing part and the brother-ness or masculinity it repre-sented. To yield in a feminine way, her poems say, is to melt, dissolve, flow away, or be transformed, and the child sought to avoid this (again, over-determined) liquid softness by fusing with hard, winged, and weaponed Mercuries (her brother) or firm old Professors with objects (her father and Freud). "Women," she wrote, "are individually seeking, as one woman, fragments of the Eternal Lover. As the Eternal Lover has been scattered or dissociated, so she in her search for him."

H.D., writes Norman Holmes Pearson, "was a very womanly woman, and her way of symbolizing what she was searching for was through males. Not the man or the flesh—I mean the principle of malehood and womanhood combined into a wholeness." [46]

As H.D. tells us quite explicitly in the analysis, she went on to transfer her baby love for her mother into a little girl's love for her father, but with the cosmic dimensions left over from her first longings still unsatisfied. Both father and mother remained for her magically, religiously, and mythically powerful. In particular, since he was an astronomer, the cosmos must have been much present in the household and the closing of distances a matter of family conversation. Because her father seemed to have such vast powers and knowledge—and symbols —the little girl's usual wish to *have* the father must have continued in its earlier, more primitive form, the wish to *be* him (as still earlier she had wished to be part of her cosmic mother with no interruptions).

To close the gap with signs. Merely stating H.D.'s myth says how being a poet, indeed, how being the particular kind of poet she was, fulfilled her personal style. Similarly, stating the myth shows the psychological basis for such literary insights as Professor Riddel's:

The threatened flower of self, caught between the great maternal oceans and the hard, firm enduring shore (the fragile flower and the stalwart tree) compose the essential landmarks of H.D.'s condition. They are the components of her recurrent myth—her *cogito*—in its purest form.

Inwardness is projected as transient and insubstantial—soft and decaying fragments of a heat oppressed space.

The poet affirms her identity not by solving the mystery but by reifying it.

But how can one locate in the stages of H.D.'s development the wellsprings of her creativity? The strong forces in H.D.'s

myth must have happened to many women: a style of mother-
ing that created "gaps," the distant father, the envied brothers.
But not every woman who experienced such a childhood became a poet. What was critical in H.D.'s life? In other words,
plenty of children experienced the "gaps"—what made H.D.
take "signs" as a way of dealing with "gaps"?

She herself told Professor Swann how much she enjoyed
as a child reading Hawthorne's *Tanglewood Tales* and Grimm
and "all fairy tales." "Perhaps, as my father and half-brother
[Eric] were astronomers the *names*, Venus, Mercury, and so
on, were subsconsciously potent." [47] But these matters are,
relative to the growth of personality, "late." All we know of
human development insists that fairy tales and the names of
planets must have taken on their importance from some still
earlier predilection for "signs."

Obviously, one does not come easily by materials from so
early in life, and only a great deal of research could tell the
full story of the poet's early development, and perhaps it cannot be wholly told even so. Yet H.D.'s memoir of her analysis
tells us a great, great deal, and "The Dream," a segment from
an unpublished series of family portraits written in 1941, adds
still more.[48]

She was born in Bethlehem—Bethlehem, Pennsylvania,
that is—then the American center for her mother's special
religion, the Moravian Church, originally called the "Unity of
Brethren" from the Latin *Unitas Fratrum*. Strongly Germanic
in its roots, it had special rituals, notably the "love feast" which
served, as Count (later Bishop) Von Zinzendorf said, to pierce
"the mystery." H.D.'s family held a central place in the sect—
they even lived on Church Street. Her grandfather headed the
Moravian seminary, and the first "signs" H.D. may have had
to adapt to were the German words her brothers and her older
relatives used. Indeed, it was while he was studying German at
her grandfather's seminary that H.D.'s father met her mother
and married her.

Her memories of her childhood are pervaded by things Germanic and Moravian—and, of course, astronomical. She remembered how her father called her "*Töcterlein*," although he was neither German nor Moravian. As an astronomer, he worked at night, which makes her think of "nightmare"— which grandfather had explained in his book *Simple Science*, which another German-speaking old Professor would also explain someday. It was her father's looking at stars that caused the family to move, when she was ten, to the University, away from the "old town" to Flower Observatory. On that move (in H.D.'s memory of it, anyway) her book of Grimm fell apart and her mother gave it away. Saying "*tempus fugit*," her father would look at stars, numbers, hieroglyphs, but not at her, although he had much to look with: lanterns, thermometers, prisms, lenses. He would go over to the Transit House at night, past the sundial that also said *tempus fugit*. Stars evidently had something to do with Time Flying, and with parting, as, so many years later, the Flying Dutchman would.

"Signs" must have meant for H.D. that warmer, more powerful unity before the move, the time of union with mother and her mother's religion and family. That world of myth and signs and language seemed to promise the omnipotence every child dreams of. "Mythology is actuality," the woman was to say, remembering Christmas in Bethlehem, when father looked at his children instead of the stars and they trimmed and decorated the *Putz* under the tree.

The "thing" was that we were creating. We were "making" a field under the tree, for the sheep. We were "making" a forest for the elk, out of small sprays of a broken pine-branch. We ourselves were "making" the Christmas-cakes. As we pressed the tin-mould of the lion or the lady into the soft dough, we were like God in the first picture in the Doré Bible who, out of chaos, created Leo or Virgo to shine forever in the heavens.

"God had made a Child and we children in return now made God; we created Him as He created us."

VIII

For H.D., as for many people, artistic creation has a religious meaning, but a secular eye can be content with a naturalistic view: the act of "making" mythological images functioned multiply within H.D.'s ego identity, her "character." For her, "signs" evidently achieved, with the least effort, the most effect in closing the gap, and she became the writer who wrote with her particular style. "Writing on the Wall," she might have called it, as she first called her memoir of Freud.

Less clear with H.D. is an additional adaptation more formal writers make: a meshing of craftsmanship (as well as the original creative impulse) with personal style so that the hard work of formally shaping the medium also satisfies multiple needs of drive and defense. Thus Wordsworth can transform the "prison," the "scanty plot" of the sonnet form into "brief solace" for those "Who had felt the weight of too much liberty." Keats can speak of poetry "chain'd" and "fetter'd" by such restraints and yet say they become the Muses' own "garland." [49] Forms in poems act like defenses in life, and defenses, as we have seen, to become part of one's style or character, must satisfy drives as well as manage them. To be a formal craftsman one must be able to satisfy drives by his very formalism. Otherwise, writing would be a misery, not (as so many creative writers describe it) a compulsive need.

H.D., however, wrote fiction and free verse, and the "form" of her poems came more from her own drives and less from a received tradition than Wordsworth's forms or Keats's. Craftsmanship there most obviously was, but of a certain kind. H.D. would set up fixed formal patterns in order to let them down. That way, she used them to create and then cross gaps. In a larger sense, H.D.'s forms involved an intense empathy with "signs" and alternations of identification and distancing rather than sharp divisions within a poem.

Nevertheless, despite the fluidity of her forms, H.D. amply demonstrates the essential thing about literary creativity: the making of poetry is simply one ego's solution to the demands set by inner and outer reality. Writing itself—even the very manner and matter—works out a personal style that pervades the multiple functioning of the ego. H.D.'s inner needs and outer realities made "signs" the way to close a gap she felt between herself and her mother, her father, her brothers, a gap in her body, in her loneliness, and so on. "Signs" evidently achieved for H.D. the most effect with the least effort and hence became part of both her character and her poetry, her lifestyle and her literary style or, in the term of Yeats's with which we began, her myth.

In another environment, storytelling, role-playing, verbal games like rhyme, play-acting, or coined languages—any of these might have proved more economical and so made for a different kind of writer. Creative writing, like any other act "in character," the selection of a vocation or avocation, wearing clothes, one's manner of speaking or walking, falling in love, getting a symptom, suicide—any human's act satisfies for him some combination of pleasure-giving and defensive needs, inner inertia and outer pressures to change, personal demands and society's stringencies. To the extent one particular activity (like writing) functions multiply for us, we become committed to it, and it takes on the status of a permanent and preferred solution. Some of those preferred solutions prove so satisfactory as to give rise to the feeling many creative writers describe of being driven, as by an inner compulsion, back to the typewriter. This, then, is the writer's demiurge, his daimon and Muse: the creative style which stabilizes the psychic economy which is his and his alone.

By comparison, how thin and unconvincing become the generalizations arrived at by averaging creative people. They fail because they do not respect the myth implicit in every human life. To be sure, creative people will "regress in the service of the ego," but so do we all, and not just to create—when we dream, when we undergo therapy, whenever we draw back into ourselves to gather resources for a new venture forward, whenever we prepare for the next cycle of "two steps forward, one step back." "Regression" explains any change and, by explaining so much, cannot explain any one person's creativity.

What about the traditional idea that the artist is mad or at least neurotic? H.D.'s account of her analysis with Freud makes it clear once more (if it is still necessary) that creativity does not come from mental illness. Neither is it a simple alternative. Rather, the key variable is *style*. Both illness (H.D's "megalomania," to take the gravest possibility) and creative writing will act out the same underlying myth. The megalomanic vision and the Imagist mythology—both will create a symbolic artifact; both will "close the gap with signs."

Her "myth" is the real explanation, not some general term that could apply to anyone. Consider the common "restitution" theory which holds that the artist re-creates symbolically what he has destroyed in his aggressive fantasies,[50] as H.D. made Freud the immortal but petrified Centurion at the gate, both dragon and dragon-killer. Indeed, one could regard H.D.'s whole *oeuvre* as an attempt to destroy and re-create her mother; but, again, we would lose all the particularity of H.D. herself and her actual creations, her bristly hedgehogs and pine trees, her blending of male and female, or her mythological quest to span the centuries with palimpsests. Further, no one can say for sure whether the next writer will match the theory, and, even if he did, we would want to know how and why his restitutions took *his* forms and not H.D.'s.

Again, we come back to the personal style and the individual life. General words like "creativity," "neurosis," or "restitution" create the illusion of laws and entities where none are. Freud explained the problem in his conclusions on the Wolf-Man case. It goes to the root of psychological explanation:

> In order to derive fresh generalizations from what has thus been established with regard to the mechanisms and instincts [in this case], it would be essential to have at one's disposal numerous cases as thoroughly and deeply analysed as the present one. But they are not easily to be had, and each of them requires years of labour. So that advances in these spheres of knowledge must necessarily be slow. There is no doubt a great temptation to content onself with "scratching" the mental surface of a number of people. . . . Practical requirements may also be adduced in favour of this procedure; but no substitute can satisfy the requirements of science.[51]

What Waelder's "principle of multiple function" and Lichtenstein's concept of an "identity theme" provide are ways of understanding terms like "creativity" or "neurosis" as functions within one deeply analyzed case rather than shallow generalizations at the mental surface of a series of "subjects."

Creativity, we can then see, is not some special, magical afflatus but a natural, logical series of solutions for some people to demands made by their inner and outer realities. H.D. found she could best meet the world by creating and becoming signs. She did so, first, by writing Imagist free verse, later by creating bounded and unbounded mythological characters. Partly because she was H.D., partly because she gained insight from Freud, she proved the paradox she so liked: mythology is actuality. Yes, she was unique and even magical, but only because she knew that she was doing what every human being does: she *was* in the way she could and had to be, in the terms of that one myth which was *her* actuality. So are we all. So do we all.

TWO

Two Readers' Minds

MYSTERIOUS OR NOT, creativity makes bright claims on us. Literary criticism, by contrast, began drearily indeed with Plato's dour insistence that literature imitated imitations, disordered the mind, and generally enfeebled men's spirits. He assumed in his indictment that he knew what literary works did to people, and so did Aristotle when he answered Plato by reassuring his own students that tragedy produced a healthy catharsis. Ever since, literary critics have gone on making a great variety of statements about literature that proceed from one or another assumption about how people respond.

The plain fact of the matter, however, is: no one, until quite recently, knew what went on in the mind of the reader because no one had a psychology adequate to the problem. Today, however, we do have such a psychology. We can know more about the writer and about the way he set down a fragment of his personal myth. By the same token, we can also know more about the reader's personal myth and we can discover from his associations with a text how he is responding to the writer's original creation. And those are the two steps this examination of two readers' minds will take.

These two readers were among a number of people who were reading poems and stories and seeing films for me as part of what, with optimism enough, might be called an experiment.[1] A group of advanced undergraduate English majors from a neighboring university agreed to act as the subjects, and each week for a period of from eight to eleven weeks, they read a story or a poem or saw a film or a play; then they met with me to discuss it in front of a tape recorder. In these interviews I tried to get them to avoid literary analysis and to talk instead about their feelings and associations to the literary works. I tried very hard not to "lead" these readers to any foreordained conclusion about what they read or general principles of reading—indeed, it was not until a long time after the interviews were over that I began to think I knew what was happening in their readings.

Each reader gave me about five hundred pages of interview material, and that was my primary evidence both for the way they were reading and for their personalities. I relied heavily on the specific words they chose, rather than turning what they said into categories or into statements about external reality which could be judged true or false. I "read" what they said, in other words, much as I would read a poem.

In addition to the interviews, they agreed to take some personality tests, which were administered, not by me, but by someone with professional experience in psychological testing. They took the familiar test in which they were asked to say what the inkblots on ten Rorschach cards could be. They took the Thematic Apperception Test in which they were shown five cards with pictures on them and asked to make up a story around each picture, saying what the situation was in the picture, what the events were that led up to it, and what the outcome would be, describing the feelings and thoughts of the characters. And, on my own, I gave them the COPE test, a brief multiple choice questionnaire which asked them to surmise the feelings of characters in certain situations. It is designed to elicit processes of defense or adaptation.

Despite these formal tests, however, I still regarded the transcriptions of the taped interviews as my primary source of information about these readers' personalities. After the interviews were over, I pored over the transcripts, trying to find the principles that related the way a reader read to his or her personality. As with H.D.'s creativity, I found the key in the concept of an identity theme or lifestyle. That is, each of us reads with a certain style, as you can see by comparing two readers' readings of the same work.

I

Sandra was a tall, very good-looking blonde, neatly and somewhat conservatively dressed.[2] She was a little shy—indeed, it was several interviews before she would look at me directly. She seemed to want the interviews to be rather fixed and rigid, and she gave me the feeling that she would have liked me to tell her exactly what to say or do in the "experiment" so that she could comply more precisely. By contrast, she had difficulty with my request that she ramble on freely and undirectedly, although in every other way she gave me a feeling of steadiness and cooperation. But we have already found other, less impressionistic ways of talking about personality.

As we saw in discussing that "one myth for every man," Heinz Lichtenstein could "transcribe" an identity theme for his patient, Anna S., as " 'being another's essence.' " I concluded that H.D. organized and dealt with her world in this lifestyle: to perceive a gap in it and then fill that gap with signs she could be or be in. I can state Sandra's identity theme the same laconic way.

She perceived the world as a kind of mystery; and sometimes by words like "trap" or "trick" she conveyed the feeling that the mystery posed dangers. If it did, she would arrange to see it no longer, vision being crucial in the way Sandra approached the world. If she found a situation promising, however, she would try to see more of it, see it from closer up, touch or even merge with it. "Promising" had special values for Sandra: it meant an equalizing of differences, a flow of power from stronger to weaker, parent to child, older to younger, male to female, or whatever. "Promising" also meant for her the simpler, earlier pleasures of nurture and food (associated, perhaps, with the stronger mother giving of herself to the weaker child). If I tried to say this in one phrase, it would be: to see and approach more and more closely and even draw upon a source of power and nurture, but not to see its loss. I cannot reproduce here all the materials from which I concluded that this myth expressed Sandra's "invariants," but perhaps it will be enough if you see her characteristic style in two of her TAT stories.

This is the story she wrote to a picture, in a sort of Thomas Hart Benton style, of a farm. A girl with books stands on the left. On the right, a woman leans against a tree—some people see her as pregnant. In the background a man is plowing a field. Sandra was asked to explain what the situation was in the picture, what the events were that led up to it, and what the outcome would be.

The picture captures Mary at a *pensive* moment. She's just about to leave for the long walk to high school where she is in the beginning of her senior year. She could have left school earlier and stayed at home to help, but she wanted to finish high school so she could leave next year and enter teacher's college. The farm hadn't always been this prosperous but had taken hard working of the rocky soil. Her brother Tom, as he grew, gave his strength to it. Father died recently, leaving Mother expecting the fifth child. She seemed to move with the seasons. "I'm different," Mary is thinking. I envy her simple life, in a way, but things will be different for me." *

Another picture in the TAT series shows a solitary boy sitting on the front step of a cabin. Ordinarily, it elicits people's feel-

---

* This punctuation is Sandra's.

ings of loneliness, loss, or depression, but Sandra supplied him with a family:

> If you walk by this hut any afternoon of the week, you'll see the boy on the stoop. His father's out in the woods working at the funny machine the boy peeked at once. All the older boys are there, too, for they're big enough to help run the machine and drive the pick-up truck to and from the hollow. Ma is working the small, dusty plot that provides a few wizened vegetables every week. She'll be back soon to start supper for the boys. He can help a little then. That's about all he can do. There aren't any other kids his age for miles. He'll just sit here and wait to grow big.

Both of Sandra's responses show the same concern with strength and work and competence—power, ultimately.

In her first story, the father had worked the rocky soil hard. Her brother gave his strength to it. Then the father died, leaving Mother expecting the fifth child—again I get the feeling there was some hard work there. Her second story, too, deals with power. Will the solitary boy in the picture grow up to be strong, to work the funny machine, and to drive the pick-up truck? In both stories, the question of strength or power involved an acute sense of the difference between men and women for Sandra. Thus, in the second, father has the funny machine and the pick-up truck. Ma has only a small, dusty plot and a few wizened vegetables. The women in both her stories have traditional roles: cook, teacher, mother.

Sandra wanted to equalize the difference between the strong and the weak or men and women, as in her first story, where Mary has to find her equivalent for her mother's fertility. Similarly, Mother's moving with the seasons matches Tom and father's working of the soil, and, in the second story, we get another cooperative venture. Father and the big boys do their bit, Mother does hers, and the little boy will wait to grow big and do his job.

This is the way Sandra wanted to see the world: as free of danger because people worked together. Each being strong, all could balance and equalize their powers. In particular, the strengths of men and women matched, then big and small, one generation and the next, and so on, including, I suppose, professor and student, experimenter and subject. Still more exactly, this equalization would take place by seeing (as, for example, the boy's peeking at the funny machine) or by touch, by moving with the soil and the seasons. In both these stories, Sandra wanted to see strong people making cooperative efforts, combining their different strengths, often in thrusting or penetrating ways, as in the plowing and fathering of the first story or driving the pick-up truck to and from the hollow in the second. These wishes of Sandra's reflect that stratum of childhood when the child's urge to "be big," to compete with his parents, his siblings, or the opposite sex, reaches a peak. Then, too, she had deeper wishes for the simple, uncomplicated nurture symbolized by food. In the most pervasive sense, Sandra wished for a mutual filling and interpenetration with power, love, and food.

Yet this mutuality had to have limits. Thus, Sandra dealt with the pictures first by treating them as isolated, special realities to be scanned visually. In her first response, she began with "The picture captures . . ." In the second, she rather self-consciously started a sort of short story based, not on Sandra, but on "you." Both her principal characters were separated from the rest of the people in the pictures. Seeing things from a distance served Sandra as a preliminary sort of defensive wariness.

If she felt insecure at that first level, she took steps to "unsee" the danger—to avoid it physically, to repress it mentally, or even to deny it perceptual entry (as by looking away). If she felt secure at that level, however, she began to seek a balancing of more important strengths through identification or interpenetration—the mutual filling which satisfied both her defensive and pleasurable needs.

This is Sandra's identity theme as it comes through in her TAT stories. When women and children have their own strengths, she seems to be saying in the second story, then things are both safe and gratifying—even in the loneliness presented by the literal picture. In her first story, when she said the deprived mother "seemed to move with the seasons," she showed both the defense and the pleasure of mutual giving of mutual strengths. Together, the mother and the seasons have strength enough to compensate even for the loss of a powerful husband; her fertility and the farm's overbalance the deficiencies it was Sandra's style to avoid.

In the course of a dozen or so interviews, however, I was able to glimpse the ways this theme permeated Sandra's perceptions of the several poems, stories, and films we talked about. Often, she would concentrate first on literary techniques to the exclusion of content, technique serving as a preliminary strength to be seen and assessed before becoming involved with the work's larger powers. Thus, thinking about Roman Polanski's *Repulsion* (a film I found utterly horrifying), she burst out: "God, wasn't that amazing? . . . . I just couldn't believe it. It had an amazingly horrifying impact, I suppose, but I was really awed by his photographic techniques." First line of defense: denial and disbelief; second, an assessment of techniques; only then, a closer contact with the film. "It was amazing that he could bring that kind of horror to the screen, I thought, and still not overdo it. Every touch was pretty perfect." She herself recognized the stages in her responses: "Most of the time I'm reading and I'm at a certain distance where I'm saying, 'Isn't this good?' 'This is really perfect here.' And I'm saying this to myself as I go along." "Then every once in a while . . . I stop saying, 'Isn't this good,' and I have a feeling that I'm moving with whatever's being said, rather than standing away and watching what's going on." Just as she had seen the pregnant mother of the first picture "move with the seasons," she spoke of herself being engrossed in a story: "It's really powerful, it's kind of a dreamy thing. It just takes you right up in it."

Strength is the key. If too much, Sandra would run away from it. If too little, she would feel repelled by the weakness. If just right, she would merge with it. Thus, she had trouble accepting the hypnotic power in Mann's "Mario and the Magician." "Just the very little bit I know about it, I had always thought that the unwillingness of a subject would prevent it. So, if that's true, then, you would have to account for it [the story] some other way, because certainly he [the hypnotist] has unwilling subjects." "You would almost have to believe that there is such a thing as power that one person could have over another person." Even so, she said, "You could reject this story on a factual basis and see it in a larger perspective of power of any one person over another person, and it becomes power of place, too, initially, before you have the magician even on the scene." Thus she had managed to synthesize the two halves of the story, the resort scenes and the hypnotist's show, around the issue that concerned her: power. But she stated it defensively, in terms of escape. "It's about freedom in very basic and important ways." She managed to enjoy the story by finding the right kind of power balance in it: "As far as the story goes, I liked, I really liked the narrator. I really enjoy his voice telling this kind of story very much." "I think it works very well, [even as] repulsive as the magician is." "They emerge as the two strongest forces in the story, and the narrator is your person to hang onto."

In the same way, she rejected an overpowering heroine of F. Scott Fitzgerald's, and with her, the story of "Winter Dreams." "It just didn't involve me to the point where I could

really care." "I don't believe in her." "It's a very simple way
to criticize it, but from all the different experiences I've had
of, oh, girls who were, quote, 'popular,' girls who were en-
chanting and mysterious in some ways, at their best, all of them
combined would never command this string of men. I don't
believe in this sort of mysterious power that she's supposed to
have." She ended her remarks on that story by contrasting it to
what was for her the right kind of relationship between a
man and a woman, which she laughingly called a "whole
theory of marriage." "I'd like to see him [the hero] and anybody else like him that's got a little bit something more than
average, find a person who has mystery, maybe, a unique at-
tractiveness . . . but only to the point where it doesn't overpower the other person." "Where each partner can kind of
meet the other one on his own ground, like where one isn't
overtaken by the other. Which wouldn't be the case if each
had his own unique qualities to begin with." And again, she
had re-created her identity theme: the balancing and exchange
of strengths.

II

To understand the inner dynamics of the literary experience, however, we need to see Sandra synthesize in some
detail something more precise than an ambiguous TAT picture. We need to see how her personal style enters into the
way she re-creates for herself a single carefully wrought literary work. Here is a poem—we have already glanced at it as
an expression of H.D.'s lifestyle of gaps and signs:

> There is a spell, for instance,
> in every sea-shell:
>
> continuous, the seathrust
> is powerless against coral,

bone, stone, marble
hewn from within by that craftsman,

the shell-fish:
oyster, clam, mollusc

is master-mason planning
the stone marvel: 10

yet that flabby, amorphous hermit
within, like the planet

senses the finite,
it limits its orbit

of being, its house,
temple, fane, shrine:

it unlocks the portals
at stated intervals:

Prompted by hunger,
it opens to the tide-flow: 20

but infinity? no,
of nothing-too-much

I sense my own limit,
my shell-jaws snap shut

at invasion of the limitless,
ocean-weight; infinite water

can not crack me, egg in egg-shell;
closed in, complete, immortal

full-circle, I know the pull
of the tide, the lull   30

as well as the moon;
the octopus-darkness

is powerless against
her cold immortality;

so I in my own way know
that the whale

can not digest me:
be firm in your own small, static, limited

orbit and the shark-jaws
of outer circumstance   40

will spit you forth:
be indigestible, hard, ungiving,

so that, living within,
you beget, self-out-of-self,

selfless,
that pearl-of-great-price.[3]

In terms of *her* lifestyle, H.D. (I think) developed the pearl as something a craftsman made, something hard, that would enable her soft self to fill a gap. Now the question is, What does Sandra do with the poem, given her rather different lifestyle? Here (with the tangles of spoken English smoothed out into written prose) is what she said. I did not, by the way, identify the author or the author's sex for her.

NNH   Well, how did you respond? What did you think of it?

SANDRA I liked it very much, right away. Even without saying it out loud, I respond to the sounds, the movement of it. It's got a fairly soft and somewhat, I suppose you'd say, undulating movement. Even the shape of the lines falls into that wave-like pattern. The sound fits in well with what he's saying, which—I'm not exactly sure if I'm holding onto all the ideas, but I

like right away the words that he's using and what he
seems to be saying. [And she giggled a little.]

NNH What does he seem to be saying?

SANDRA Well, it's something about the way people make their
worlds or their own private little worlds, and how
much you'll be open and maybe let the world come
in, and how much you're going to close yourself off.
This, "I sense my own limit." Exactly what he means
by not wanting or by not worrying about infinite
water—I'm not sure. It seems somehow that he's got
a confidence in whatever there is in himself. [Pause.]
I'm not really sure if the thought is really changing
him or not. [Pause.] Probably not, because he seems
to be saying, "Hold on to whatever that unyielding
thing inside of you is," and which he—what she *
calls the "pearl-of-great-price" at the end. It seems to
be something that you really won't get from outside.
It's got to be made inside of you and very much your
own. And that really is the major thing. You know.
It's the most important thing that you have.

NNH Are there any phrases that appeal to you particularly?

SANDRA I was interested in the way that he starts out talking
about the "seathrust . . . against coral." It's a strong
image of the power of water, moving in towards
what's, you know, against the shore, like a coral reef,
which is likewise, you know, a really strong and
hard object for it to hit again, as opposed to, say,
sand. And then further down, he talks about the pull
of the tide which is just really as powerful a thing,
but it's working just the other way. And it's interesting that he ties it in . . . with the moon and the
moon being, well, traditionally a feminine thing. He
uses the word "her" (for the moon) which in my

* Note the slip.

mind makes the magnetic or the outer pulling, the tide pulling, a sort of a feminine feeling, where the really aggressive "seathrust" seems masculine or very aggressive as opposed to the sort of *beckoning* influence of tide.

NNH   What about, in that case, "the octopus-darkness"? Just down from "the tide." If the "seathrust" feels sort of masculine and the pull of the tide—what?— more attenuated or feminine or something, how about "the octopus-darkness"? Where does—

SANDRA   That's supposed to be like the antagonist of that one bright cold spot of the moon. And I suppose it's supposed to be a dark end, the kind of thing that would just devour—that seems like it . . . could just devour and engulf the moon, but the moon is so unyielding in her own way, that even this (which is a pretty unpleasant image, "octopus-darkness," I think) . . . [is] certainly, you know, a powerful thing. [Her voice fell.] Let me think of all the things about octopi [and she laughed]. So it makes the moon stand out as amazingly strong and—

NNH   Suppose I asked you if you could just sort of run down through the poem, picking up words or phrases that intrigued you. . . . I was very struck, for example, by the way you put the moon against "the octopus-darkness," which, you know, seems very sensible, but it hadn't occurred to me before.

SANDRA   I like the first line right there, "the spell in every sea-shell." I respond saying, "Yeah, that's right," you know. I think first of the kind of shell that you hold up to your ear, which certainly has a spell. I think of the kind of shells that are enclosed in— Kind of spiral inside. That kind, you know, an open shell. I think that's what he means, the kind of open shell that looks kind of mysterious because you know an animal was in it, or something might still be there. "The seathrust . . . against coral"—I suppose it's interesting because he says it's powerless against coral, because you think of the immense strength of—and you know, this is a very strong word—and then you think of the immense hardness of coral. So that's quite an impact there. "Bone, stone, marble" . . . to me, they appeal more soundwise. [And she stopped.]

NNH   You don't have to do everything, just do what catches your eye.

SANDRA   The "flabby, amorphous hermit"—that's kind of good, talking about the animal that's inside "its orbit of being." And then he uses interesting words just to take the shell beyond shells where you know that he's talking about something more than [and her voice fell again] crabs or something. [Laughing] Of course, I know it would remind you of, you know, "Build thee more stately mansions, O my soul."

NNH   What's that from?

SANDRA   Oliver Wendell Holmes.

NNH   Oh, of course! "The Chambered Nautilus."

SANDRA   "It opens to the tide-flow." This "tide-flow," I suppose, is kind of—yeah, it's got to be an *in*coming tide, a flowing tide. It's a much gentler thing than the wave, "seathrust." It's sort of a creeping thing, and I suppose this is what, it says here, bring[s] the fish its food. I don't know. I won't stop to worry about exactly what parallel it has to the human soul [laughing]. "Nothing too much." Who was it that used to say, "Nothing too much"? Socrates?

NNH   Aristotle.

SANDRA   Aristotle?

NNH   A Greek, anyway.

SANDRA   That's interesting. "I sense my own . . ." This is the
point where it changes to the first person. "My shell-
jaws." That's very interesting, to put in a— taking
[it] into the realm of a human voice and then having
it be "shell-jaws." I don't know if I think "egg in
egg-shell" fits too much. I suppose it reinforces the
idea he's trying to get at, but if I were writing, I
wouldn't put it in, because I think he's got enough
to work with—the sea words and the shell words. But
it does give a good picture of—you know—[how]
completely filled it is. And then the next part that
really gets me is this about the moon, those good
words used there, "the pull of the tide, the lull," "the
moon," "the octopus-darkness" (that is what we just
talked about).

This sounds strange, that he would say, "Be
firm in your own small, static, limited orbit and the
shark-jaws of outer circumstance will spit you
forth." I'm not sure if this doesn't change the tone of
the poem, because these are the kind of words that—
People don't usually tell you to "set your own very
static—" "Static," of course is a word that might
have negative overtones, although maybe he's just
saying, "This is honestly the way it is. If you're very
careful and if you just set your own boundaries,
you're going to be a lot better off." Certainly a lot
of people write this way, too, in the sense that maybe
they've tried not having boundaries and it turns out
that it doesn't do you any good, so it's just a warning. It's kind of a bitter thing, I suppose.

NNH   Do you like that? Does that statement make you
feel good or not so good? "Be firm in your own small,
static, limited . . ."

SANDRA   I can say "Yes" to it in a way, because I can say, I know what that feeling is like, at certain times, when you *will* say to yourself, "That's it. I'm never going to try doing anything anymore. It just gets me into trouble." You know. "Forget it. You just try to do something and the world just jumps right on you." So, for a while, you say, "That's it," but then it doesn't, for me, it doesn't last, and for most people probably it doesn't. And certain[ly], I'm sure, not for anybody that's creative like this poet is, because I think that he's ending up saying something. Boy! I wish I knew exactly what he *was* saying [and she giggled].

NNH   Well, can I behave like a literary critic and suggest that the poem has three sections? [In] the first part he's talking about the outer boundary that the shellfish sets for itself by the shell that it grows. Then, in the second part, where, as you point out, it goes from the third person to the first person, "*I* sense my own limit," and so on. As it were, "the flabby, amorphous hermit" describes "the flabby, amorphous hermit" sitting within this shell, and that goes all the way up till practically the end. . . . "Be firm in *your* own small, static, limited orbit" (which is the shell still). "Be indigestible, hard, ungiving," and *this* is the shift, "so that, living within, *you* beget, self-out-of-self . . . that pearl-of-great-price," where it's now the hermit talking, not about the hard thing that it makes outside of itself, but the hard thing that it generates within itself, which I thought you were referring to when you said this was the most precious thing, the best thing that you have.

SANDRA   Yeah, that's what he seems to be saying. I suppose. I can't see—

NNH   [*in furore critico*] Well, think about it as a poem

about the creation of the poem itself—in other words, the poem being the pearl of great price.

SANDRA   Yeah, but I still don't understand. . . . What's the shell, really you know? Is that the traditional way that you would cut yourself off from whatever is outside? Because a poet can't do that really for very long. Maybe he doesn't mean, you know—

NNH   Well . . . "it unlocks the portals at stated intervals: prompted by hunger, it opens to the tide-flow." [And our discussion turned to my interpretation and other poems by H.D.]

I find it intriguing that Sandra associated Holmes's "The Chambered Nautilus" to this poem, for H.D. had mentioned that poem as one of her favorites in talking about immortality and Freud. Everything else Sandra said about this poem, however, seemed quite different from H.D.'s characteristic concerns. Sandra interpreted the images in terms of strength and power. She found an interaction of male and female in the poem, and she also talked about it in terms of enclosure and fitting in and cutting oneself off. She wanted to ward off the infinite, but she did not like the idea of being isolated from reality entirely as the last lines seem to me to suggest. All this is very different from H.D.'s associations to seashells in *Tribute to Freud:* "the abstract idea of immortality, of the personal soul's existence in some form or other, after it has shed the outworn or outgrown body." And it also differs from some of what I take to be the poem's plain prose sense. We are seeing Sandra achieve the poem for herself in her individual style.

III

From the study of several readers like Sandra reading many particular works, I have derived four closely meshed principles that I think govern the way a reader re-creates a literary work. First, there is one general, overarching law: *style creates itself*. The reader tries, as he proceeds through the work, to compose from it a literary experience in his particular lifestyle. In particular, line by line and episode by episode, he responds positively to those elements that, at any given point in the work, he perceives as acting out what he would characteristically expect from another being in such circumstances. What cannot be perceived as acting out his expectations he responds negatively or remains indifferent to.

To respond positively, to gratify expectations this way, a reader must be able to create his characteristic modes of adaptation and defense from the words he is reading. This is the second principle, and the most exacting: *defense must match defense*. For a reader to take pleasure from a reading, he has to protect that pleasure. He must re-create for himself from the text rather precisely all or part of the structures by which he wards off anxiety in real life. It is as though the text can enter the subterranean depths of his mind only to the extent he has exactly shaped it to pass through a tunnel. Once he has done so, however, the subterranean chamber turns out to be large and open. The reader can very freely shape for himself from the literary materials he has admitted a fantasy that gives him pleasure, and this is the third principle. He projects into the work a fantasy that yields the pleasure he characteristically seeks. Another analogy to the reading experience might be a party where the invitations are carefully scrutinized to see that they match the list, but once in, the guests behave in a pleasantly rowdy and uninhibited way.

A fourth principle, however, puts a limit and justification on the rowdiness. The reader "makes sense" of the text: he transforms the fantasy he has projected into it by means of the defensive structures he has created from it to arrive at an intellectual or moral "point" in what he has read. Thus the reader comes full circle. In reading, as in life, he transforms his fantasies into socially and personally acceptable modes of being, but in reading, as contrasted to life, he derives the materials he transforms, not from experience, but from the words and stringencies of a literary work. Style creates itself.

Sandra's first move, then, must have been to create from this poem her characteristic ways of warding off anxieties that might interfere with her pleasure in it. She found danger in the possibility that the interpenetration she sought and the mutual filling with power, love, and food could become overwhelming and engulfing. Partly, then, she defended by setting limits. The interactions she wanted had to be not too little, and particularly, in the Delphic motto she recalled, "Nothing too much." She objected to the image of the eggshell: "If I were writing, I wouldn't put it in, because I think he's got enough to work with." "Exactly what he means by not wanting or by not worrying about infinite water—I'm not sure." It was typical of her to imagine a danger as, "You just try to do something and the world just jumps right on you." Confronted with such a subjection, she might, she said, withdraw and say, "That's it. I'm never going to try doing anything anymore." But she could not deal with a threat for long by withdrawing into a shell or any other "traditional way that you would cut yourself off from whatever is outside." "For me, it does not last." That is, she would need another defense, one that would permit an interaction of mutual strengths.

She demonstrated this other pattern, more satisfactory for her, in dealing with what she called "a pretty unpleasant image." The "octopus-darkness," she said, was "supposed to be like the antagonist of that one bright cold spot of the moon . . . the kind of thing that . . . could just devour and engulf the moon, but the moon is so unyielding in her own way that even this . . . unpleasant image . . . [becomes] a powerful thing." In other words, the moon, by being strong, enabled Sandra to take pleasure in the unpleasant image of the octopus. Conversely, the octopus "makes the moon stand out as amazingly strong." In other words, if each is strong, each makes the other strong.

Then, since she did not entirely trust this adaptation, she sought limits in another interaction: "Let me think of all the things about octopi" in reality. Thus, Sandra doubly refused the idea of cutting oneself off; instead she wanted to adapt both to reality and to the poem by interacting with them as long as she felt confident of her own strength. She became quite selective in composing this defense from the poem. She rejected the egg image and the word "static" as providing too little interaction. She was "not sure" about "infinite water," though; it would provide too much. In most of the poem, she did find just the balance of strengths she sought.

Once she had constructed her characteristic adaptive strategy this way, she could project her preferred fantasy into the poem very freely. Sandra wanted both to be and to interact with a source of strength and nurture. From an adaptive point of view, she avoided dangers and coped with reality this way. From the point of view of fantasy, she achieved gratification by the same strategy. Thus she created a poet for this poem who was himself safe and solid, someone she could rely on, someone rather like herself. "He's got a confidence in whatever there is inside himself." Then she developed two specific aspects of her basic fantasy of a mutual filling.

The first involved having things inside yourself, and she interpreted the whole poem along these lines, although I'm not sure she could have produced much textual evidence to support her reading. The poet did not need to worry about "infinite water," because of this "confidence" in "whatever there is in himself." "He seems to be saying, 'Hold on to whatever that unyielding thing inside of you is,' and which he . . . calls the 'pearl-of-great-price' at the end. It seems to be something that you really won't get from outside. It's got to be made inside of you and very much your own. And that really is the major thing. . . . It's the most important thing that you have," she said, shifting from "he" to "you" and so both being and interacting with strength. The eggshell image works only to the extent it gives "a good picture of . . . [how] completely filled it is." The shell itself "looks kind of mysterious because you know an animal was in it, or something might still be there." She changed a phrasing: instead of saying the animal "senses the finite, / it limits its orbit / of being, its house," she said, "That's kind of good, talking about the animal that's inside 'its orbit of being.'" Sandra liked having and making things inside, but in order to meet the world with inner strength, not to isolate oneself.

What you have inside is "the most important thing" because it permits these interactions of strength, and they were the real gratification she fantasied. "Seathrust" is "interesting because he says it's powerless against coral, because you think of the immense strength of . . . the immense hardness of coral. So that's quite an impact there." "It's a strong image of the power of water, moving in . . . against the shore, like a coral reef, which is . . . a really strong and hard object for it to hit again." "The pull of the tide . . . is just really as powerful a thing, but it's working just the other way." Then she went on to note that the poem uses "her" for the moon, "which in my mind makes the magnetic or the outer pulling, the tide pulling, a sort of a feminine feeling, where the really aggressive 'seathrust' seems masculine or very aggressive as opposed to the sort of *beckoning* influence of tide."

What we know of human development would suggest that Sandra's fantasies about male and female interaction as the balancing of strengths derived from still earlier fantasies about being fed. She decided the "tide-flow" was feminine, beckoning and pulling. Also, "It's got to be an *in*coming tide, a flowing tide. It's a much gentler thing than the wave, 'seathrust.'

It's sort of a creeping thing, and . . . [brings] the fish its food." I find it intriguing that Sandra promoted the "flabby" mollusc into a firmer, stronger "fish"—again, this is typical of the way a reader, once he has been able to match his defensive strategies, very freely re-creates the poem to give himself the kind of pleasure from fantasy that matters *to him;* here, a momentary hint of ithyphallic power.

Sandra, however, did not settle for mere fantasy: she transformed the fantasies she projected into the work by means of the defensive and adaptive strategies she had built up from it, and so made esthetic, intellectual, and moral "sense" of it. Thus she interpreted the sound pattern as part of an interpenetration: "It's got a fairly soft and . . . undulating movement. Even the shape of the lines falls into that wave-like pattern. The sound fits in well with what he's saying." Even if she didn't really mean this statement and just thought sound would be a good thing to mention to a professor of English, she was nevertheless telling me that when she thought about sound, she saw and felt it interacting with the visual shape and verbal content of the lines. She had created an esthetic version of her basic wish.

At a more intellectual level, she urged the poem toward a theme. "He uses interesting words just to take the shell beyond shells where you know that he's talking about something more than crabs or something," and then she linked the poem to "Build thee more stately mansions, O my soul," vaguely trying to find a "parallel" between the "fish" and the "human soul." "Nothing too much" occurred to her as another possibility. And like a more professional critic, she attributed all these themes to the poet or the poem, not to her own synthesis.

All these "themes," however, really represent Sandra's own efforts to bring the poem to human size and strength, the very efforts that gave direction and insight to her interpretation. For example, she was able to spot what amounts to an

error in the poem (or, at least, something rather odd that
neither I nor any of the other readers mentioned). She referred to line 23: "This is the point where it changes to the
first person. 'My shell-jaws.' That's very interesting . . . taking it into the realm of a human voice and then having it be
'shell-jaws.' " The mixed metaphor stood out for her because
she wanted to see humans, males and females, not molluscs.

Similarly, when I asked her to pick out words or phrases
that "intrigued" her, she immediately said, "I like the first line
right there. . . . I respond saying, 'Yeah, that's right,' you
know." Yet when she said out loud what she was responding
to, she phrased it simply, "the spell in every shell" so as to
emphasize the matching of the *-ell* sounds. She had disposed of
the "for instance," which suggests to me an unfamiliar, unknown dependency on something that has gone before. She replaced that dependency with an interaction she knew: "I think
first of the kind of shell that you hold up to your ear, which
certainly has a spell," and thus she created a mutuality where
none had been. Again, in fleshing out the word "sea-shell," she
(quite legitimately) gave it her own meaning: "I think of the
kind of shells that are . . . spiral inside . . . the kind of open
shell that looks kind of mysterious because you know an animal was in it, or something might still be there." Similarly, she
picked out "the seathrust . . . against coral," which she liked
for a combination of reasons—but to which she also gave her
specific interpretation: there was "quite an impact there."

In short, Sandra, as she read the poem, went through a
continuous process of making the poem her own, by fleshing
out generic words with her specific interpretations, by bringing her associations and wishes to bear, and by emphasizing
those elements that fitted her synthesis and putting aside those
that didn't. All this continuous creation of the poem went into
her arriving at a value judgment and also a meaning.

Sandra's most complete statement of theme was her first

decision that the poem was "about the way people make . . . their own private little worlds, and how much you'll be open and maybe let the world come in, and how much you're going to close yourself off." This seems a perfectly sensible reading to me, and also one which quite reflects Sandra's personal style. She therefore liked those sections of the poem that had to do with the sea entering and feeding, but she did not like the ending: "I'm not sure if this doesn't change the tone of the poem." " 'Static' . . . is a word that might have negative overtones." And despite my clumsy efforts to get her to see the poem my way, as a study of creativity, she did not like a theme "that you would cut yourself off from whatever is outside." That could not be a transformation of *her* fantasies and adaptive strategies, and only if a reader can achieve a transformation of unconscious into conscious content that fits his lifestyle will style have found itself. Only then can the reader have a positive experience of the literary work.

It is important to recognize that the four principles governing the literary experience come full circle so that one becomes "locked in" to a positive experience and "locked out" of a negative one. Having created his characteristic defensive structures from the work, the reader has warded off anxiety. He can therefore project into it the fantasies that give him pleasure, and he can use his defenses to transform the fantasies into themes that give the work intellectual cohesion and sense. Having achieved this transformation, his style has indeed created itself: as he goes through the work line by line, he finds in it characters, episodes, images, ideas, all acting out his characteristic expectancies for them. At this point, he can perceive no difference between the processes "in" him and what he sees "in" the work, and he finds that special sense of absorption or merger that literary experiences can give us.

"I lose track of time." "I am attentive and absorbed, unaware of surroundings." "Total anaesthesia." "A sort of

drugged or fascinated absorption." "I feel 'taken out' of myself." The experience is a familiar one—most people have it
with movies, television, or easy fiction. Harder literature
usually requires an effort that keeps one aware of oneself.
Sandra is the only reader I have ever worked with who became "absorbed" in poetry or difficult prose such as Henry
James's, perhaps because she used attention to technique to
avoid being taken over by a fictional reality that could be too
big and strong. I think when Sandra first talked about "There
is a spell," she was responding to this kind of absorption: "I
liked it very much, right away. Even without saying it out
loud, I respond to the sounds, the movement of it. It's got a
fairly soft and . . . undulating movement." I am reminded
of the way she described the fertile mother in her first TAT
story: "She seemed to move with the seasons."

I think her image of moving together is her way of describing the feeling of no difference between self and work;
she is saying the boundaries have come down between self and
other. One has a feeling of union and merger, a loss of self-
consciousness. Robert Gorham Davis has phrased this deeper
sensation and the mechanism behind it quite beautifully:

When a man is "absorbed" or "immersed" in a story . . . he is not
primarily thinking *about* what he reads. That implies separation,
externality. The work, rather, is thinking *him*. His ego has become
object, not subject. We speak of being "absorbed" and "immersed"
in the work, but actually it is the other way around: we take the
work into ourselves, introject it. What the ego is immersed in—
sometimes with oceanic raptness—is its own larger, profounder self,
which the work, as a series of excitations and counterexcitations
has set in motion and directed.[4]

In technical terms, we introject the literary work. We create
in ourselves a psychological transformation, which feels as
though it were "in" the work or, more exactly, neither "out
there" nor "in here" but in some undifferentiated "either."

I say "undifferentiated" because the process involves a sense of the boundaries blurring between self and other, a feeling of merger which derives ultimately from a recreation of that same symbiotic at-oneness with the giving mother that we have seen in H.D.'s analysis. Psychoanalysts, following Ernst Kris, used to call a healthy loss of a sense of reality (as in reading) a "regression in the service of the ego," but Roy Schafer has recently made that phrase more precise by separating those ego functions that persist from those that do not. "The change occurs in an aspect of thought that is prerequisite to any reality testing, though its presence is usually only implied. The change is in the representation of . . . oneself as thinker of the thought" —one ceases to think of oneself as dreaming the daydream, hallucinating the hallucination, reading the novel, or seeing the movie. "There is only suspension of the reflective self representation that pertains to the act in question." [5] To gain pleasure, one suspends one's representation of oneself reading. In being gratified by reading (as by dreaming), we merge with the source of gratification as once feeding child and nurturing mother formed a unit. For example, we can speak of someone as a "voracious" reader, "insatiable," a science-fiction "addict," or "hungry" for detective stories. We might say someone else has better "taste" but that most people take any old "pap" the "tube" feeds them. Bacon's well-known aphorism carries on the same analogy: "Some books are to be tasted, others to be swallowed, and some few to be chewed and digested." In other words, we take in literary works and make them part of our psychological workings as we make food part of our digestive processes.

At least we do that when the work in fact succeeds in gratifying us; but, of course, there is a whole range of success and failure. The reader may be able to build up his psychological processes from the work completely, or only partially, or not at all. He may lack the skills to do so, or he may be confronting a work which has features he simply cannot accept as part of his psychic functioning and still be dealing with something which is recognizably the literary work. For a positive reading experience, style must create itself. But that does not always happen, and it did not with our second reader, Saul.

IV

Saul seemed a serious young man whose impressive hairiness did not make me think he was defying anything: it simply demonstrated his concentration on the important things, instead of mere appearances.[6] He conveyed an inwardness that had gained him a reputation among other students for scholarly intensity and intellectual commitment. Often speaking so softly no one else could hear him, he seemed focused on his own affairs, only occasionally becoming animated or involved with others. Toward me, the professor, the experimenter, he was very wary indeed, particularly when I would press him for easygoing, rambling talk about what he had read. Then he would turn back to the exact words in the text, reading them rapidly into his beard, as if to himself, to bear out the interpretation he was developing (although he rarely brought any of these interpretations to a final form).

Saul, one could say, was much concerned with self-possession, yet his self-contained quality involved a number of paradoxes. Although he was the most scholarly of the readers I worked with, he was also the most original and idiosyncratic. He sought a precision and clarity far beyond anything the others tried for, yet more often than not the result was shadowy, vague, and elusive. He seemed eager to participate in the project, but when it came to the interviews themselves he so managed and controlled them that he became, in effect, quite uncooperative. He talked, but he seemed to talk mostly to himself.

I took Saul's inwardness and scholarly intensity to represent at the visible level a deeper, inner need to hold knowledge and situations in himself. Saul was a remarkably guarded and secretive young man. At his deepest level, he seemed most to fear being a small, passive object with some big, vague power threatening to take something out of him. Saul's scholarly and logical search for precision was the creative way he avoided this danger. He constantly searched his environment like a photographer or a systems analyst for anything big or vague that might pose the danger he had to avoid. He needed to see all threats before they could get too big; to leave nothing hidden or uncertain; to control situations; and, in particular, to hew to measured balances between such poles as closeness and distance, emotions and intellect, acceptance and rejection, or man and woman. He became an intellectual who got things to fit or match in an exact balance that he could control. He bargained terms with that potentially superior force, fearing a disproportion that would lead to an unequal bargain and a situation where he would be overpowered and forced to give up something precious. If he could not control matters by such a match or bargain, he would avoid the whole situation, psychically or physically, and look for a world of safe precision elsewhere.

If I tried to generalize Saul's solutions to these inner and outer demands as an identity theme, I would put it in the following sentence: because he perceived the world as forces trying to control him, he tried in turn to bargain out of those forces a defined control that would not overpower him. Finally, he searched the world for controls that he could himself control.

Saul thus resembled Sandra in that he was guarded, circumspect, and much concerned with balance; but, as we shall see, he differed from her in just those particulars that should throw our four principles into high relief. Saul brought quite a different style to these questions of balance and equalizing. Sandra was concerned with balancing through mutuality and interpenetration. She perceived the world in images of intrusion and inclusion. Saul was less concerned with boundaries between people, more uneasy about his own boundaries and the way they might be affected along the one issue of control. Who controls whom? Who is bigger and more mysterious? Who is small and precise? Who will be hard and who will force the other to yield something soft and sloppy? These were the questions that bothered him, and, fearing control in the experiment, he became almost explicitly uncooperative, even in the relatively uncontrolled task of writing TAT stories. Here are the two Saul wrote that correspond to Sandra's.

Terrible.
    Terrible—boring picture—sloppy emotions—cheap women's mag story, or maybe cheap teenage girls' magazine
    2 sisters—older has her strong, handsome man, now carrying his
∧ child. Strong, dominant, sensual and *uses* it—American bitch-goddess—looks satisfied
    Younger—still in school (books) or perhaps teaches—kind of the White Virgin to her sister's Dark Woman, but more than symbol—I suspect hung up that she isn't as good w. men, but a bit appalled at her sister's manipulative methods—thus the (sloppy) look of dismay on her face.

family

    Appalachia—boy's ∧ not desperately poor (he has shirt, overalls in decent repair) but still they live in hand-hewn house. Poor enough that the boy is succumbing to the emotional blight that poverty confers on the inhabitants of the other America. Boy's unhappiness partly this, partly his *father's absence*—he has been gone, looking for work, for a month (when the mines pulled out 3 years ago, dad lost job)—father not broken yet by the poverty (only extreme last 3 yrs) but affected. The boy is affected by father's progressive demoralization.

In his first "story," Saul simply rejected (or fled) the whole thing as being sloppy, vague, or sentimental—this is his fear of the indefinite. At the same time, he put in the imagery of a bargain with words like the repeated "cheap" or the half-remembered phrase, the "bitch-goddess success." He spoke of the sister as a controlling force, a woman who "uses" her sensuality, who is "manipulative." She "has" her man and is "now carrying his child." Saul often saw the controlling forces he feared as women.

It is part of his flight from this first story that he saw no details at all, but turned the characters into symbols of dominance or exploitation, "strong, handsome man," "Dark Woman," and the rest. He set up a sort of balancing, where the older sister has the man and the young one has books and a sense of values. But the older one wins: she can manipulate men and so forces a sloppy look of dismay out of her younger sister.

In the second picture, he paid much more attention to detail—apparently he felt he could tell how good the boy's overalls were or how the house was made. Again, however, he brought in loss, absence, poverty, just the opposite of Sandra, who populated this picture with mom, dad, and a whole set of brothers, to say nothing of wizened vegetables and a pick-up truck going to and from a hollow. Saul saw a large, vague, superior force: "poverty," he called it, using that word only but using it twice. "Poverty" was attacking an equally large, vague victim, "Appalachia," "the other America," and dealing out nebulous harms, "emotional blight," "progressive demoralization." The specific people are—vaguely—"succumbing" or "affected."

Against shapeless ills, Saul tried to balance things and set limits, as in his careful appraisal of the shirt, the overalls, and the house. He carefully distinguished two different causes for the boy's unhappiness. The family was "not desperately poor." The father was "not broken yet." The poverty had been "extreme" only the last "3" years (expressed with a digit) since the mines left. He drew similar elusive distinctions even in his rejection of the first picture. "Cheap women's mag story, or maybe cheap teenage girls' magazine." Saul asserts but then hedges, qualifies, redefines. He made the younger sister into a symbol "but more than symbol." In the first picture, he played off Dark Woman against White Virgin, this latter lady hung up on the one hand *but* appalled on the other. "But" was an important word for Saul, a word that enabled him to assert something *but* then cut it back to the right size.

Where Sandra liked stories by finding in them a source of strength she could focus on, usually a male character or narrator, Saul sought precision in language. "The prose works with authority and precision," he said of an author he liked, "specifies something." "I like the precision in defining this emotion with a good deal of— Well, after 'precision,' I don't know for sure what to say. 'That strikes me as absolutely right.' That's another way of saying 'precision.'" "'Crystalline' is another word." "I get back to these vague critical terms like 'conciseness' and 'efficiency' and so forth, which I groove on."

Indeed, Saul became so concerned with his own precision that he would say very little on his own behalf in the interviews. Mostly he would read from the text we were discussing. As a result, for all his admiration of the exact, he himself remained rather shadowy and elusive. He seemed to fear having something very precious to him forced out or taken away (as the "mines" were pulled out in his second story). Thus he could say of a character disillusioned at the end of a story that "he gives it [his dream] up or has it yanked out or whatever." He came in one day with "one of the most marvelous pieces of graffiti that's ever been around." "'Born a virgin, lived a virgin, died a virgin, laid in the grave.'" Maybe the reason Saul found it so funny was because it acted out on someone else (particularly the kind of withholding woman he resented) his own basic fear: that something would be forced out of him that he could not limit or control.

Saul tried to meet this danger by finding precise terms of exchange, in politics, in literature, and in his work with me. Alas, he could not find them in "There is a spell." In Saul's reaction, the first thing we see is total defense. He fled any kind of relationship at all to the poem, just as he got angry at the first TAT picture.

NNH   Listen, to shift gears, can I try a poem on you? Just out of the blue? [Saul read "There is a spell" for some minutes.] I don't know whether you've ever encountered this before or not. I don't have any structured set of questions. How does the thing make you *feel*? What sort of—

SAUL   I would expect this thing in *The New York Times*, for instance, on the editorial page, or something like that. I'm not sure the *Times* does that, but that sort of on-the-newspaper, on the *Courier-Express*, or *Express* editorial page. Um. Well, not quite. Um. It just generally doesn't move me either way. It doesn't do anything to me.

NNH   Do you s—

SAUL   (Interrupting.) "Is master-mason planning / the stone marvel: / yet that flabby, amorphous hermit / within, like the planet—" [He reads this quickly, mumblingly.] It's a *bad* poem—I mean, with me in my strongest reaction.

NNH   "It's a *bad* poem." Why? What's wrong?

SAUL   Let me see. Um. Well, um, he's playing with: the self is shelled in, is walled in. (Mumbling.) "Continuous, the seathrust / is powerless against coral—" Just some things. "Master-mason planning / the stone marvel: /

yet that flabby, amorphous hermit / within, like the
planet / senses the finite—" Talking like a graduate
student again. [We laughed.] "Infinity." The infinity
and the finite, throwing in these words. Things like
"I sense my own limit."

NNH   What about "I sensed [*sic*] my own limit"?

SAUL   Well, that's—

NNH   I take it, it's producing a negative response from you.

SAUL   I really don't finally have much specific to say, because the poem doesn't do much of anything specific
to me. I don't think— There isn't much specific about
it— This is my Pound thing working, where— Well,
it's a mixture of some sketchy, kind of abstract-in-the-
way-people-who-don't-know-much-about-philosophy-
but-try-to-use-it way. Its power. "The octopus darkness / is powerless against / her cold immortality."
This kind of meaningless abstraction is— "Her cold
immortality"—whatever that means.

NNH   Well, I take it, it would mean the full circle of the
shell, wouldn't it? I suppose. "Infinite water / can not
crack me, egg in egg-shell; / closed in, complete, immortal / full-circle," and so on. I take it that's what
"cold immortality" refers to. What about the image of
the—whatever the shellfish is—"oyster, clam, mollusc / is master-mason planning / the stone marvel"?
The idea of the oyster, whatever, as a builder of some
sort?

SAUL   [After a long pause] Oh, basically no reaction.

NNH   No reaction.

SAUL   Um. [Long pause. Then we both laughed.]

NNH   Blank, huh? Are there any images that you *like* in it?
I mean, you've pointed to some lines you *don't* like—

SAUL   Well, one more thing I don't like, in the fifth-to-the-
last stanza, suddenly, like the editorial page poems,

begins to preach: "Be firm in your own small, static, limited / orbit and the shark-jaws / of outer circumstance—" Oo-oo-h, "the shark-jaws of—" I can imagine Karl Mundt saying that one [and we laughed], whom I just perceive, understand I have a chance to vote against next fall. Karl Mundt is running for reelection this fall and my voting address is still South Dakota. I'm very happy about that. [He read mumblingly again.] Hauls out the clichés. He's trying to do something slightly different with it, I think, but the same meaning. "Be indigestible, hard, ungiving." Yeah, I don't find— If there's anything I tend to like, it's that "Be indigestible, hard, ungiving." It crashes with "pearl-of-great-price." But the last five—well, the last five lines except for the last one, I tend to like. One can be— One can turn to the reader, one can't put on that—what is it? the grammar term that escapes me?— one can turn and preach, or turn and say, um—

NNH   Imperative?

SAUL   Imperative. Yeah, imperative. —can do that as long as one is not being too gospelly about it. One of Anne Sexton's—[his tongue got twisted, and he repeated]— Anne Sexton's best poems does that. Now the sense of it is that I think she's talking to herself somehow. Perhaps in some schizophrenic way or perhaps in just some rhetorical way. Not clear. Get on your donkey and ride, or whatever it is, that's all. Get out of this place any way possible.

NNH   Well, I'm sorry it doesn't do anything for you.

Saul virtually rejected the poem outright, except for the one small section he liked. In that one segment, however, he demonstrated the overarching principle of response: that a reader will react favorably to those elements that do within the work what the reader himself hopes for toward any separate entity. Saul thought it very important that he be able to establish the terms of control himself. He singled out the last lines of the poem: "If there's anything I tend to like, it's that 'Be indigestible, hard, ungiving.'" And if there was anything Saul was, it was "indigestible, hard, ungiving"—toward me, the TAT, and the poem as a whole. No one was to get anything out of anyone, unless he, Saul, said so. He accepted all the lines which (at least when I read them) are the most tightly end-stopped of all: "Be indigestible . . . hard . . . ungiving . . . so that . . . living within . . . you beget . . . self-out-of-self . . . selfless." He rejected only the last, flowing phrase, "pearl-of-great-price," which had vague, religious echoes and dealt, not with creation or control within the body as such, but the thing created or controlled.

Just as Sandra liked this poem in her own way, Saul disliked it in terms of his character and lifestyle. He could not use the poem to create his adaptive strategies toward the world. That is, he tried to deal with the possibility of vague threats in the world by allying himself to the precise and the measurable. In poetry, this became his "Pound thing," that is, Pound's famous call for precision in the Imagist manifesto (and, interestingly enough, Pound had said H.D. exactly fitted the creed). Saul, however, complained about this poem, "There isn't much specific about it." It has "meaningless abstraction." It "hauls out the clichés." He contemptuously singled out phrases like "flabby, amorphous hermit," which he quoted twice, or "The infinity and the finite, throwing in these words." It was out of his need to avoid larger controlling forces that he criticized the poem for being "gospelly" and preaching. The religious images are not without significance in Saul's world of large, vague forces; neither is his forgetting the word "imperative."

Thus, when we hear Saul repeatedly say things like "It

doesn't do anything to me," we should recognize that he is partly reassuring himself. "It just generally doesn't move me either way." The bargain became quite explicit when he said, "I really don't finally have much specific to say, because the poem doesn't do much of anything specific to me. . . . There isn't much specific about it," and therefore he could not let it do anything to him. I find it amusing that I fell right into Saul's defensive patterns: irritated somewhat by his insistence that he had no reaction and no understanding of the poem, I gave him a testy, overbearing explication of a few lines, which led in turn to his flat rejection not only of the poem but of me. By his long silence he won, and all I could do was laughingly acknowledge that he had in fact won.

Just as he rejected my control, he rejected the control even of the Anne Sexton poem he liked: he could stand its preaching because it said, "Get on your donkey and ride" (and, given the level of Saul's fantasies and defenses, he may have made it a pun on "ass"). That escape was only one of several, however, beginning with his displacing attention from the poem to *The New York Times* or a Buffalo newspaper, to graduate students, to Pound, to Karl Mundt, or to Anne Sexton. Changing the subject enabled him to flee or, more exactly, banish what he perceived as a vague attempt to control him.

The one thing he could accept was the section of the poem that acted out his own adaptive strategy: "Be indigestible, hard, ungiving." Even there, he had to assert control by disapproving of the last line, "that pearl-of-great-price." To this limited extent he was able to achieve in the poem a transformation of his fantasies about giving out or holding in by means of his adaptive strategy of establishing precise controls to arrive at a theme: "He's playing with: the self is shelled in, is walled in." To this limited extent, Saul's character structure, which would seem almost to rule out any possibility of his ever enjoying a

poem in a simple, immediate way, allowed him to compose the
kind of inner transformation which is the poetic experience.

V

The precondition for that experience is that the reader
build for himself out of the raw materials of the work his
particular pattern of adaptation and defense. If he cannot or
will not, then he can have no positive experience of the work,
as Saul could not re-create from words like "flabby, amorphous
hermit," "finite," or "infinity," the precision he needed to feel
secure. By contrast, he could find his characteristic adaptation
in being "indigestible, hard, ungiving." Similarly, Sandra could
re-create her adaptation, the balancing of strengths, by interpreting the poem as male and female interpenetrations or by
seeing the sound mesh with the content and the "shape of the
lines." Her adaptations required that she see the poem in terms
of being open and letting the world come in—she could not
accept the poem when she thought it spoke of closing oneself
off. Saul was just the opposite: he had to have the poem deal
with the way the self is "shelled in, is walled in," and he could
not tolerate the vague, planetary interactions.

If a reader has re-created his defensive pattern from the
words and constraints of the work, he continues his positive
experience by projecting a fantasy into the work, that is, a
cluster of unconscious wishes derived from one of the developmental periods of childhood. This distinctly does not mean
that a poem is simply a congress of phallic and feminine symbols. The fantasy or, more typically, fantasies we experience as
its core can deal with all kinds of childhood issues, themes of
power or of giving and getting or of taking into and putting
out of the body as well as the familiar rivalry of the child with
his parent of the same sex. Further, literary experiences do not
come simply from fantasies but from fantasies transformed.

We seek a sense and coherence, and we find two agents

that transform fantasies so they will yield us the esthetic, social, moral, and intellectual significances we demand. One such agent is meaning, but one must think of it as a participle rather than a gerund, a process instead of its end product, a defensive or adaptive strategy rather like sublimation. Using symbolic transformations, say, of a seashell, the fantasy at the heart of a poetic experience loses some of its infantile and primitive quality and becomes an adult and sophisticated concern with artistic creation or immortality or an ethical position of withdrawal. The second agent is form, by which I mean all the choices one makes to manage the fantasy material: omissions, orderings, and juxtapositions in the broadest sense as well as particular tones and stresses and stanzas and rhythms. In a literary context, we are accustomed to calling these things literary "form," but in a psychological sense they act like the whole human range of defensive and adaptive strategies.

Finally, if we are, as we usually phrase it, "absorbed" in the literary experience, we feel no boundary between ourselves and the literary work. It yields us pleasure, and it makes no demands on us that we act on the real world outside our symbiotic relationship with itself. Thus the literary situation (particularly its theatrical form) draws on a whole sequence of past experiences of real or imagined gratifications coupled with inaction: all kinds of nurture, artistic pleasures reaching back to being read to as a child, dreaming—a most important version of this experience—and, the root of it all, the experience of passively being fed by a loving mother.

In short, the literary experience consists of introjecting the work and thereby transforming a fantasy by means of form and the process of meaning toward a conscious coherence of esthetic shape and significance. This is the so-called "transformation" model of literary experience first set out in *The Dynamics of Literary Response*.[7] Later work with real readers like Saul and Sandra confirms this model but issues an important reminder: this transformation does not take place in literary works but in the people who read them. Poems do not, after all, fantasy; people do. Novels do not embody defensive strategies; people find them in novels. Meaning—whether we are talking simply of putting black marks together to form words or the much more complex process of putting words together to form themes—does not inhere in the words-on-the-page but, like beauty, in the eye of the beholder.

More exactly, this transformation happens in a space which reader and work create together. The reader reconstructs, as we have seen, part of his characteristic pattern of adaptive or defensive strategies from the work, and this re-creation must be rather delicately and exactly made. Once he has done so, however, he can admit through the filter of his particular style some or all of the work, which then becomes the material from which he very freely creates the kind of fantasy that is important to him. He then (again, with great freedom) transforms that fantasy by means of the defensive strategies he has created toward the coherence and significance he consciously demands. Altogether, then, he has duplicated his own style of mind. Neither he nor we can see any difference between his characteristic mental processes and those that seemingly belong to the work. The question "Where is the fantasy and defense, in the work or in the reader?" ceases to have any meaning.

The reader is a re-maker of the poem, just as the writer is its maker. H.D. had in her head some transformation of unconscious material when she wrote "There is a spell," perhaps associations like those she recorded in *Tribute to Freud*, that to work with Freud was to reach "the high-water mark of achievement," to "crown all my other personal contacts and relationships, justify all the spiral-like meanderings of my mind and body." As she wrote, she recalled lines from Oliver Wendell Holmes's "The Chambered Nautilus": "Till thou at length art free, / Leaving thine outgrown shell by life's unresting sea!" In particular, the famous "Build thee more stately mansions, O my soul," seemed to refer to what she and the Professor were building between them.

Sandra, too, thought of the Holmes line in her re-creation of "There is a spell," yet I do not think that H.D. in the slightest sense "communicated" the reference to Sandra. Rather, the re-maker of "There is a spell" associated that line from a schoolgirl's reading to the image of the seashell, just as the original maker of the poem did. The poet does not speak to the reader directly so much as give the reader materials from which to achieve the poem in his own style. Thus, Sandra created from the poem a theme of the mutual interpenetration of man and woman; and, to be sure, a seashell is a classical feminine symbol to those who would use Freud as a decoding machine. But the sea which penetrates the shell is hardly a masculine symbol, and neither H.D. nor Saul seem to have been affected at all by the "universal symbolism" of the seashell. Saul read the poem quite differently: the only part of it he could give life to was the command to "be . . . hard, ungiving, / so that . . . you beget, self-out-of-self, / selfless." Saul read the poem in terms of his more wary style, keeping things within himself against coercions, an identity theme which was neither H.D.'s nor Sandra's. Indeed, the only part of the poem Saul could like was the part Sandra singled out to *dis*like.

In short, the maker of a literary work and every re-maker create their own work in their own style of mind, and we come again to the paradox with which this book began. We, as humans, live in a world which is both objective and subjective, a world where, in some way we have not yet understood, we are able to share subjectivities which remain nevertheless completely private and individual. Nowhere is this puzzle more familiar and commonplace than in the world of letters. The student of literature, the teacher, the critic, and every member of an audience live with a consensus of shared esthetic experiences which, however, never lose their personal, idiosyncratic quality. A reader re-creates a literary work so as to re-enact his own character—as the late Stanley Edgar Hyman aptly put it, each reader "poems his own poem"—and now we know four principles by which he does so.

The next question is: How do different readers build a bridge from one reading to another so as to form a community of shared experiences which keep, even so, their very private status? We need to look to the basic principles which govern the interaction of one mind with another, and we can most precisely approach these large issues through the two minds we have here and now, as it were, yours and mine.

THREE

My Mind and Yours

USING PSYCHOANALYSIS to look at two readers' minds seems to have cast us adrift in a sea of subjectivity, a most uncomfortable place for a critic in this last third of the twentieth century. If literary studies of the past forty or fifty years have made one great achievement, it is the careful "objective" study of the literary work as a thing in itself. This formalist or "new" or textual criticism made possible a teaching of literature quite different from the morocco-bound and old-madeiraed musings of the nineteenth-century literary panjandrums. Looking closely at the text led to a sharing in the broadest sense, a democratizing of experiences that had formerly been reserved for the few, as well as a new firmness in judgment and interpretation.

Now, however, Sandra's and Saul's comments on "There is a spell" suggest that all that objectivity was illusory: what really determines the kind of reading a work gets is not the words-on-the-page but the ego style of the reader. The poet is left with no magical powers at all, only the most limited control over the reader's response. A democracy of letters becomes an anarchy in which one reading is as good as another, and nobody can claim a more valid interpretation than anybody else. Each reading becomes private and personal, ultimately un-

√ person of importance

sharable and untestable. A single poem thus turns into as many poems as there are readers. Or so it would seem.

To explore the subjectivity of response or, more exactly, its sharability, I am going to introduce a third reader of "There is a spell," this time a professional, me. I shall begin the same way Saul and Sandra did, avoiding intellectual interpretation.

I

If I simply recount my feelings toward the poem and the associations it evokes, I find that I like those sections of the poem that link the shellfish to larger, cosmic beings. I enjoy the internal rhymes and echoes in the poem, particularly "spell" and "shell" in the opening stanza, "bone" and stone" in the third, and "self-out-of-self / selfless," near the end. The poem's lists have for me a kind of stately, processional quality, "coral, bone, stone, marble," or "oyster, clam, mollusc." In the "for instance" of the first line, I feel the resonance of a human being reciting to me or presenting a formal argument.

Much of what pleases me in the poem, though, is simply the talk about seashells, which never fail to delight me. Although I am no collector, I have often bought shells at seaside shops, to use as a paperweight or simply to leave around on a coffee table to be looked at and handled. I am fascinated by the cellular but mineral hardness and the pattern of annular growth like tree rings, the slow accretion of an exotic and improbable splash of color or (especially) a severely geometric shape. I half-remember articles I have read, linking the shapes of seashells to logarithmic spirals and Fibonacci series, and H.D. reminds me here that it is a senseless, shapeless blob of an animal who achieves such a "stone marvel" as a chambered nautilus. I delight in her conceit that he is a "craftsman" and "master-mason." If only the repairmen my house keeps needing were as docile, skillful, inexpensive, and quiet as oyster, clam, or mollusc.

I find myself drawn most strongly to those parts of this poem where the smaller geometry of the shell is echoed in larger geometric or even cosmic forces. I relish words like "planet," "orbit," "finite," "ocean-weight," "moon," and "darkness." Conversely, I do not enjoy phrases that take that larger geometry and turn it into a threatening, bestial environment. I find myself strongly objecting (like Saul) to the moralizing in the phrase "shark-jaws of outer circumstances" and questioning if it is anatomically possible for whales to swallow molluscs and spit them up again. In general, I resent the last section with its counsel to be firm and ungiving, and I find the last phrase, "pearl-of-great-price," evasive of both the moral and poetic responsibility to come to a precise conclusion.

If I try to systematize my reaction, I find myself approving those sections of the poem that evoke in me a sense of geometric intelligence and a participation in the larger geometry of the cosmos, particularly as a reaction against something "flabby, amorphous," fleshly, and human. I find myself disliking eggs, whales, sharks, and octopus, as against planets, orbits, or circles. I like the points of relatedness in the poem, and dislike unrelatedness. I distinctly react against the shift in the last section from a grammatical third person relating to large cosmic forces and holding his own, to a first person counseling a second in a smarmy scoutmasterish way to "be firm."

Still more generally, as I look back over what I have written, I see that I have repeatedly substituted the abstract, general, cosmic, or universal for the organic, eating-and-being-eaten, personal, and human (even, or especially, the mason who has so repeatedly and expensively failed to repair my front steps!). Thus, in reading the poem, I have also read myself. I am, I believe, a person who would like to master the inside relationships of things by knowledge or vision but who, at the same time, feels his identity preserved in staying on the outside.

Thus, I like the parts of this poem that I can interpret in terms of knowledge and vision—the geometry and growth associated with the outsides of molluscs, their stone shells. I like the transmutation of the flabby inside to the generalized and abstracted outside. I find myself preferring images to which I can have an external, abstract relation over images which threaten to involve me in an inside where identities are engulfed or eaten.

In general, my style is to seek greater and greater generality, but the poem converges into a smaller and smaller radius. Thus, I like the first section most: it seems to generalize and expand the situation of the shellfish. I interpret the second part as arguing that the mollusc should be complete in itself, and I find that mode less pleasing. Finally, the last section argues that one should turn inward, and I find this least satisfactory because it urges a position which is not powerful and not outside. I can accept it to the extent it refers to "you," not me, but I still don't like it.

As my treating the poem in three sections shows, however, I am not responding to it in a completely subjective, intuitive way. I also respond to it as a professional reader, a critic and teacher using what discipline, skill, and experience I have. As a professional, the first and most basic question I ask myself is, How can I interrelate all the different details of the poem? This, to me, is the fundamental task of the literary critic, and it is one that all readers almost automatically set themselves. Certainly Saul and Sandra did.

For me, a great deal of this poem comes together around the theme of boundaries. In a literal way, the whole poem says, "if you create an outer boundary, you achieve security against outer forces so that you can create within." That "you," however, masks over one of the boundaries within the poem. That is, as I argued to Sandra, I see it in three discrete sections: lines 1–22 which are written in the third person about the shellfish; lines 23–37 which speak in the first person—"I sense my

own limit," "I in my own way know"; and lines 38–46 which
address "you."

To my abstracting eye, size also marks off these three
sections. The last part deals with things inside, smaller than the
shellfish. The middle section deals with animal-sized things.
True, they vary from mollusc and egg to whale and octopus
and even on to "limitless ocean-weight; infinite water" (although this is surely hyperbole—the distance is the depth of
the ocean, not infinity). Even so, these are distances that have
to do with life on earth, unlike the distances in the first part
of the poem which go beyond "the planet" which "senses the
finite" and "limits its orbit," distances astronomical in size, ap-
proaching the "infinity" which would be "too much" compared to the earthly "tide-flow." Associated with this first,
largest section are words like "spell," "marvel," "temple, fane,
shrine," or "hermit," with religious dimensions. Scallop-shell,
egg, and pearl can all serve as symbols for the Virgin (although
I do not know if I would have noticed this in the poem if I
were not already aware of H.D.'s interest in mythological and
religious signs).

I sense the importance of boundaries in still another way,
by lists like "coral, / bone, stone, marble," or "house, / temple
fane, shrine." The beginning and end of such a list constitutes
a boundary, and I would expect those boundaries to coincide
with the stanza or line boundaries within the poem. Here they
do not coincide, and I find myself made more sharply aware of
the whole question of where one stanza leaves off and another
begins. Consider the sequence of phrases in the sentence which
says the water

> can not crack me, egg in egg-shell;
> closed in, complete, immortal
>
> full circle, I know the pull
> of the tide . . .

Although a semicolon marks off the egg from the "full circle," they could equally well be appositives connected by commas. The sentences run into one another in sense (if not punctuation) with no clear semantic boundary, especially none that coincides with line or stanza divisions.

As against these fluid boundaries, the plain sense of the poem urges "you" to set boundaries up, and many words and phrases, like "be firm" or "unlocks," presuppose the existence of definite limits. This is a poem that lets me find plenty of boundaries in its form—a boundary every two lines, in fact. Yet the poem sloshes over these boundaries with run-on sentences, phrases carrying across from one stanza or line to the next, and overlapping lists, until the last half-dozen lines. Then it firmly imposes limits, even within lines, as it tells us to do. Read aloud, those last lines sound this way to my ear: Be indigestible . . . hard . . . ungiving . . . so that . . . living within . . . You beget . . . self-out-of-self . . . selfless . . . that pearl-of-great-price.

In its larger, structural form, I find each of the poem's three phases starts small, opens up, and then closes down again. The first begins with "it," the tiny animal inside a seashell, but enlarges it to a planet in its orbit, and then closes down again at line 22 with "nothing-too-much." The second begins there, in the first person now ("*I* sense *my* own limit"), but compares that tiny me to the moon in the octopus-darkness and then clamps down again with the reassurance that "the whale cannot digest me" at line 37. Finally, the third section deals with "you," tells *you* to be firm so you will be safe against the vast, abstract "outer circumstance," and then it clamps down again with the tight phrasings of the last half-dozen lines. In form, then, as well as content, the poem, as I re-create it for myself, lets the boundaries down and sets them up again.

In short, in my experience of it, the poem comes together around twinned themes of creation and dependency, both com-

prised in the single idea of boundaries. Dependency makes one
vulnerable to threats from outside. Against them one sets up a
definition of self created from within like a seashell, but outside the self. Then that first act of creation permits another, a
still more beautiful creation, like a pearl, inside. In other words,
if you set up barriers to hold off threats from outside, you
achieve both an inner security and a magical power to create
a double beauty, a beautiful boundary outside like a seashell or
inside like a pearl. And, of course, the poem (read this way)
matches H.D.'s general pattern: to perceive the relation between oneself and the world as a gap; then, isolated, to create—
or even be—the beautiful thing that fills the gap. Further, this
central theme brings into a coherent whole even such oddities
in the poem as the "for instance" of the first stanza and the
"pearl-of-great-price" of the last. Each reaches out beyond this
poem to something else, either the poem before this in the
cycle of *The Walls Do Not Fall* or the riches of reference and
symbolism in the Biblical echo. Thus each calls attention to a
boundary while it breaches it—as indeed the whole poem does
and the act of creation must always do.

To me, developing various themes and images toward a
central focus this way constitutes a satisfactory analysis of the
poem as a thing in itself. This is what regular, formalist, or
"new" critics do. I am also, however, a psychoanalytic critic,
tempted toward another mode of reading besides textual analysis or an impressionistic account of my feelings. I like to hold
concepts derived from psychoanalytic experience up to literary
works and see relationships.

When I do that with "There is a spell," I find it coincides
quite strikingly with certain clinical phenomena. That is, when
someone compares himself (in a dream, say, or his free associations) to something like a shellfish or an insect, particularly a
tiny animal which is, as it were, "all mouth," he is almost certainly drawing on fantasies, themes, or issues from that first

chapter of infancy when the mouth was our chief way to meet the world. We hungered. We wanted to take things into ourselves, and the boundaries between inside and outside, self and other, little child and big mother, had not yet firmed. The mouth, in effect, served as the flexible boundary between a proto-self and another who came and went, came and went.

When its mother was present, the small infant felt sated and merged with the large source of his food and love (the experience we have in a muted way when, as adults, we become "absorbed" in works of art). Alternatively, when she was away and he had to wait and endure frustration, he had to realize that he could not fuse, that that huge source was another being, that therefore he himself was. It was through the mouth, then, and out of the rhythmic cycles of hungering and being fed by another that each human being set up his identity theme and his awareness of his small self as a separate entity. Derivatives of this early separation and reunion in feeding play a prominent part in situations all through life of giving and getting, which, depending on the style the individual brings to them, can be loving and merging or aggressive and biting—as in this poem.

H.D.'s shellfish nourishes itself from the rhythmic going away and coming back of the "tide-flow," but that vast, powerful sea also threatens "invasion," "thrust," "crack," and "pull," so that the mollusc has to safeguard itself by its hard, stone shell. "Prompted by hunger," it opens to the nurturing other but avoids being engulfed and overwhelmed: "My shell-jaws snap shut." One's own hunger, after all, is the sign that the other also hungers and could eat you up. The stronger and greedier your own appetite, the more you must fear any appetite that could engulf, overwhelm, or devour you. And, indeed, as I look for this fantasy in "There is a spell," I find that it is precisely when the shellfish is prompted by its own hunger to open to the tide-flow that it must fear invasion by the infinite.

One can resist that danger by closing one's mouth, denying or limiting one's hunger, and concentrating on a life and creation completely within. When the mollusc establishes its own limit, when it is firm in its small, static, limited orbit, then it is safe. The whale cannot digest it. The shark-jaws of outer circumstance will spit it forth. Its isolated safety defines another sort of identity, "self-out-of-self, selfless," a denial of the mutuality from which a true self comes. Thus I discover here together three "oral" themes often seen together in non-literary contexts: eating and being eaten, opening and closing the boundaries of self, juxtaposing the vast and the tiny.

I see other fantasies here also. Once it is secure, the shell-fish can create a body product within itself, self out of self, a pearl of great price. That image, read with a clinical eye, comes from the child's next stage, when he relates to his parents through the creations of his own body about which adults care so much—both positively and negatively. They may be precious. They may be part of self or not. They may be "living within" or dead matter. And all these issues can be found in the last five lines that Saul singled out. One can also find in the poem images and themes from the third stage of child development, when the value attributed earlier to receiving love and nurture, then to producing something precious or disgusting, becomes attached to the question of gender: Does one have something "flabby, amorphous" or something "hard," "firm," "bone," or "stone"? Something which penetrates or something which is penetrated (like a seashell, that feminine symbol)? Can one make a precious something inside one's body (as a mother can)? Or does one try for an infinity outside (like H.D.'s astronomer-father)?

One can find fantasies from all the levels of child development in this poem. In life, they would be transforms of one another, the later growing from the earlier, and one is tempted to say they are transforms in the poem too. The early question of opening or not opening to be fed underlies later fantasies about opening to give up a precious object from inside one's body or being a male thrusting outward against an infolding, penetrable female. Equally, I am tempted to say the poem transforms these unconscious, infantile fantasies linked to the stages of child development toward an esthetic or intellectual "point."

Poems do not, however, have fantasies or transform them toward themes—people do. Seashells do not symbolize women on paper—only in someone's mind. By the same token, poems mean only when people find meaning in them. The words on the page are simply so many black specks until someone who speaks their language comes along to give them life. They do not have patterns or interrelations or themes except as someone achieves them in and through the poem. And neither formal critical analysis nor a psychoanalytic interpretation as such tells how a reader makes the poem into a poem.

II

An account of one's feelings, a formal explication, a reading through specialized knowledge (here of "orality")—in treating these three as distinct ways of reading "There is a spell," I have put asunder what human nature joins together. When someone talks or writes about a poem, all these ways of looking at it come tumbling in at once. Naturally. For each in its own way expresses the reader's personality.

When someone responds to a new experience (poetic or any other kind), he does so by means of the personality and previous experience he brings to it. All these ways of looking at a poem (even the most "objective") serve as ways for the reader to take hold of this experience, hence as part of his ego's characteristic way of dealing with reality, and therefore as expressions of his identity theme. And this is true no less for the professional reader than for the two students. Inevitably, "the poem" I read is "the poem *I* read," and the "I" in that sentence is best described by an identity theme like those I outlined for Sandra and Saul.

I suggested above that my identity theme had to do with preserving a sense of self and securing self-esteem by gaining power over relations between things, in particular, mastering them by knowing or seeing them from outside rather than being actually in the relationships. For example, I like to work with photographs and movies because they are all surface. I have already suggested ways in which my "gut reaction" to the poem expresses this identity theme. I like the parts of the poem that describe abstract and astronomical relations, objects with visible forms and no interiors, like geometric figures ("orbit," "circle," "stated intervals"). I like, too, the resonances, lists, and connections leading to generality which link the various themes of the poem in a fairly abstract way.

It is not surprising, though, that simple preferences should follow a persistent ego style. It is somewhat more unexpected to find that the specialized knowledge one brings to bear on a poem does, but such knowledge serves almost like a free association. The reminiscence of Oliver Wendell Holmes's "The Chambered Nautilus" meant so little to me that it slipped my mind, although I knew of it from working with H.D.'s *Tribute to Freud*. Yet Holmes's poem served Sandra as an association which let her satisfy her need to promote the seashell and the mollusc into stronger and more important things —humans and souls.

The specialized knowledge I thought relevant was psychoanalytic experience with the eat-or-be-eaten fears of earliest childhood and later nightmares which led me to other psychoanalytic observations of the stage when the boundaries of self are being established by waiting for nurture and taking it in. Again, then, I was associating to the poem in terms of inside and outside. Another psychoanalytic critic, less concerned with that polarity, might give more importance to the way the sea pervades the poem and talk about what Freud called the "oceanic" sense of fusion (also associated with the symbiosis of mother and child in infancy). Still another psychoanalytic commentator might stress the last section of the poem as a fantasy of creating something hard and precious inside the body the way a child is begotten (and we know this theme would have had special importance for H.D.). Indeed, a group of psychoanalysts to whom I presented this poem and Sandra's response to it concentrated on the seashell as a feminine symbol and the command to "beget" a pearl. They decided both poem and response involved pregnancy fantasies.

Other readers might bring to bear a knowledge of religious or mythological symbology (which had importance for H.D., as we know from Chapter I). Still other readers would no doubt bring yet different kinds of special knowledge to bear, other biographical information about H.D. perhaps, or historical data about the trends toward mythology and symbolism in Anglo-American poetry during the nineteen-forties. A Marxist would inquire into the "conditions of production" of the poem. Sandra interpreted the withdrawal of the last lines (which did not suit her identity theme at all) in the light of her own theory of poetic creation: that the poet has to draw on experience and reality for his inspiration.

In short, the knowledge one brings to bear on a poem derives from a personal style just as much as preferences do. What is surprising to me—and troubling—is the discovery that my critical method, disciplined, professional, accredited, also acts out my identity theme. I *like* examining the verbal surface of a text, looking particularly for an "organic unity" in the way the parts all come together. From the very first evening I encountered it, the new criticism has exerted almost a spell on me. I found compelling and attractive the idea of analyzing the words on the page and them alone. The demand that one treat the poem as a thing in itself referring only to itself and hence that one pay no more attention than absolutely necessary to historical background, evaluation, or author's biography or intention suits me exactly. I took pride and pleasure in seeing this approach dominate more and more academic departments of literature, first in America, then England, now on the continent.

Conversely, it has been hard for me to look at what goes on "inside" readers instead of simply confining my attention to the surface of the text and presupposing a response to it. I have been pried loose from such a simple credo, however, by repeatedly bumping up against one salient fact. Wherever one exchanges critical interpretations—in the classroom, learned journals, literary quarterlies, professional meetings, or casual conversation—one finds that different readers read differently and there seems to be no way of laying the differences to rest.

For example, I interpreted "There is a spell" through a theme of boundaries. Again, I was concerned with seeing the way things came together, particularly with their retaining or losing their separateness, keeping their insides together or apart. Saul interpreted the poem in terms of a withholding self; Sandra said it had to do with an opening and admitting self. They also were expressing their ego styles.

Particular insights and interpretations, too, proceed from habitual patterns of ego choices. For example, I noticed that I, like Sandra, automatically assumed the shell in this poem to be something beautiful and special, not an ordinary clam or oyster shell. In terms of the text, we credited the word "marvel" more than the list of its possible craftsmen ("oyster, clam, mollusc"). Although Sandra arrived at the same result, presumably she did so because she wanted to create equal balances of power and beauty—the shell had to be as important an object as the sea. My valuation of the shell, however, proceeded from my general tendency to give special weight to the external geometry of things and situations. She with her interest in finding human interactions in the poem noticed the inconsistency of having a human "I" refer to "my shell-jaws." I, with my concern for patterns of opening and closing, did not. Concentrating on size relationships was another way I made the details of the poem interrelate geometrically, and my view that the poem has three movements of opening and closing affirms boundaries and separateness—outside-ness, if you will—still another way.

One could go on, but the point must be abundantly clear by now. Each of us reads in his own characteristic way—that is, as an expression of his particular identity theme, just as each of us has his own way of walking, speaking, joking, driving, smoking, making love, or looking at a landscape. This reading style is deeply engrained, more deeply than even a professional's training as a reader. Far from changing one's reading style, critical skills, specialized knowledge, and the experience of many books will all serve as ways of fulfilling it and carrying it into practice.

Nevertheless, despite the individuality of the reading experience, there *is* consensus. Notice that all three readers of "There is a spell" arrived at much the same central theme for the poem. Saul said,

He's playing with: the self is shelled in, is walled in.

Although he found the poem's handling of the problem of control unsatisfactory, Saul oriented even his negative experience toward what he cared about both unconsciously and consciously. He found in the poem a central theme of rejecting control from outside, and he emphasized the idea of withholding and withdrawal, being shelled or walled in.

Sandra stated the theme this way:

It's something about the way people make their worlds or their own private little worlds, and how much you'll be open and maybe

let the world come in, and how much you're going to close yourself off.

She worked out a theme in terms of her concern with the interpenetration and giving of private strengths. The reversal and
shift to "you" in her phrasing suggests how much such an ar-
ticulating of theme had to do with herself and her own conscious and unconscious values, her preference for a "you" who
lets "the world" come in as against "people" with "their own
private little worlds," and the doubling of "worlds" carried out
her need to balance and equalize.

The third reader—to keep to the convention among
psychologists of calling subjects Ss, we could name the third
reader Seymour—emphasized the distinction between inside
and outside:

If you set up barriers to hold off threats from outside, you achieve
both an inner security and a magical power to create a double
beauty, a beautiful boundary outside like a seashell or inside like
a pearl.

He stresses separateness, abstract relationships to be looked at,
and the mastery of interpenetrations—as we have seen.

This consensus does not come about simply because the
poem "caused" it, but because the three readers all took some
of the same elements from the poem to make up their individual syntheses: a seashell, a force invading it from without,
and a resistance from within. For Saul, the important thing was
the resistance. For Seymour, it was the boundary that faced
both outward and inward. For Sandra, it was letting the
world in. Even these minima, however, took on different values
for different readers.

The true picture of the consensus must begin, not with
the poem, not even the bare essentials of the poem, but with
the reader. He reaches into the poem and takes material from
it with which to achieve an experience within the character-

istic pattern of ego choices he uses to minimize anxiety and cope with reality. We have seen four principles at work. He uses his skill at reading to achieve all or part of his pre-existing adaptive strategy. Once defended this way, he can freely absorb materials from the poem with which to build the kind of pleasure-giving fantasy that counts for him. And he uses the adaptations he has synthesized to transform that fantasy toward an esthetic or intellectual "point." Thus his style creates itself in the poem. The reason we see consensus is *not* because the poem evokes the same experience in different readers—it doesn't. We see consensus because different readers are using the same material.

Each reader is like a later civilization using the resources left by an earlier one. Often, in Greece, one encounters a building that has gone through such a re-creation. The original Greek architect left behind him a classic temple and thought his work finished. With the coming of Christianity, however, new worshippers would convert his Aphrodites to Marys, his Apollos to Christs, and the golden rectangle of his foundation to nave and narthex. If Turk or Saracen took the building over, different remodelings occurred: the graven images were taken away entirely and the classical triangles became domed and half-domed to admit another kind of religious experience. To argue which—mosque, church, or temple—is "the real one" is idle. Each conception was valid for those who made and used it; each was what current planning jargon calls a "worship facility," although, to be sure, one came first, one made the others possible, and elements of that first one are used to make the later versions.

Nevertheless, the only thing the building *is* in any permanent sense is a pile of stones, as a poem *is* the words-on-the-page. Different builders can assemble the same stones into a building in many different ways, with more and less violence to the raw materials, just as different readers can construct different experiences of a poem, with more and less contortion of the words and the plain sense.

Further, it is not a case of a logical, rational apprehension of the true classic temple as classic temple upset and distorted by later ages of religious and political passion. Each successive architect marshaled all his skill and knowledge to serve that single conception of the building which combined his esthetic and his cultural values. So with the poem. One does not read critically by resisting personal and emotional tendencies to distort. That approach comes from a false notion, that there is some Platonic idea of a given poem which is corrupted by the imperfect human act of reading it. Hence, the best reading is that which is most impersonal and objective. The trouble is, reading can never be impersonal or objective. Critical skills serve a total conception of the poem rooted in the reader's character, drawing on all kinds of values and experiences which grow from the same deep roots in him.

The same empirical observation rules out the concept of poetry as communication. In no way can the idea of a poem as a fixed message from poet to reader explain the relationship between different readers' readings or between the poet's conception and any reader's. Interpretation is not decoding. Each reader constructs meaning as part of his own artistic experience. He achieves the work for himself through his own system of skills and values and thereby justifies and coheres his response. He does not recover some pre-existing intention latent in the work as a "message."

By the same token, the maker cannot impose his meaning on any reader who does not wish to accept it. He can only exclude certain possibilities by the choices he makes which limit for once and for all the raw materials from which his audience will create its experience. Not even the doughtiest Islamic conqueror could turn a classic temple into an igloo or a wickiup. The poet, however, working with words, not stones, is not so secure. He cannot prevent bizarre reworkings, although the reader might have to do violence to the text or ignore it to force them out. Even without wrenching, the reader has lots of range. He could read "There is a spell" as referring to the most rare and gorgeous whelk or the most prosaic quahog, although he would have to torture or turn away from the poem to make it refer to ham sandwiches and hay.

In short, one can truly say that the theme or content of a poem (as against the mere words on the page) has to be something one can achieve with a minimum of shoving, heaving, and hauling of the actual words. Even this minimal statement, however, does not go beyond the level of mere opinion—one man's heave is another's gentle nudge. And this most negative and limited assertion of an objective content still tells us nothing about the way readers arrive in a positive, creative way at consensus about a given poem.

III

I would like to explore the connection between Saul's and Sandra's and Seymour's readings, the interrelation ultimately between my mind and yours, by starting fresh, with another poem, one about which there is little, if any, consensus. I (or Seymour) found it at first quite inexplicable and yet, when I recognized in the last lines whom it concerned, incredibly moving. I would like to ask you if you can assent, not to my feelings about this poem, but my interpretation. Here is the poem:

THE DAY LADY DIED

It is 12:20 in New York a Friday
three days after Bastille day, yes
it is 1959 and I go get a shoeshine
because I will get off the 4:19 in Easthampton

at 7:15 and then go straight to dinner
and I don't know the people who will feed me

I walk up the muggy street beginning to sun
and have a hamburger and a malted and buy
an ugly NEW WORLD WRITING to see what the poets
in Ghana are doing these days
                              I go on to the bank
and Miss Stillwagon (first name Linda I once heard)
doesn't even look up my balance for once in her life
and in the GOLDEN GRIFFIN I get a little Verlaine
for Patsy with drawings by Bonnard although I do
think of Hesiod, trans. Richmond Lattimore or
Brendan Behan's new play or *Le Balcon* or *Les Nègres*
of Genet, but I don't, I stick with Verlaine
after practically going to sleep with quandariness

and for Mike I just stroll into the PARK LANE
Liquor Store and ask for a bottle of Strega and
then I go back where I came from to 6th Avenue
and the tobacconist in the Ziegfeld Theatre and
casually ask for a carton of Gauloises and a carton
of Picayunes, and a NEW YORK POST with her face on it

and I am sweating a lot by now and thinking of
leaning on the john door in the 5 SPOT
while she whispered a song along the keyboard
to Mal Waldron and everyone and I stopped breathing [1]

I find those last lines, the last two especially, and the final "I
stopped breathing" almost staggering in their impact. Yet I
find the details of the poet, Frank O'Hara's, life, his shoeshine
and his adventures in the Long Island Rail Road and the 58th
Street bookshop and liquor store irritating because they seem
so random and inconsequential. Knowing me, I could say

as Freud said, "Some rationalistic, or perhaps analytic, turn of mind in me rebels against being moved by a thing without knowing why I am thus affected and what it is that affects me." Of such sentiments are literary critics made—"Critics are occupationally disposed to write most about what puzzles them most," says Northrop Frye—and I find it amusing that Freud made this confession in introducing a short venture into criticism which he thought so purely esthetic a "love-child" as to be illegitimate material for a psychoanalytic journal to publish.[2]

Some people may be able to make sense out of "The Day Lady Died" as a portrait of life in artistic circles in Manhattan in 1959. Some may find it sufficiently justified as an elegy for someone black, female, and a great artist. Others may see it as a poem about political oppression, the Bastille echoed in the last years of Billie Holiday's life. As for me, I can only make sense of such a poem by trying to bring all its puzzling elements into some fairly tight relation.

The one critical comment I found on it was Paul Carroll's: he argued that any such quest for unity would be quite useless, that this poem's images occur without any organic reason, and that that is the poem's chief virtue. It is like an action painting: the poem *is* the act of writing it and nothing more.[3] Now I think that is a good way of making sense out of those oddly casual images—for some people. It pleased me to see this 1959 poem connected to the movement of action painting contemporary with it, but that connection wasn't enough to assuage my annoyance at the indifference and contempt toward the reader implied by the self-centered doings of the first twenty-four lines.

I first tried to deal with the randomness of those images by bringing a psychoanalytic concept to bear. Prompted by the line, "I don't know the people who will feed me," I began to think about the poem in terms of that same fantasy of taking in from another that I found important in "There is a spell" and the phenomenon of literary absorption. "Taking in" inter-related for me the hamburger and malted and also the liquor and cigarettes, particularly the flavorful and pungent brands O'Hara singled out (and which this ex-smoker tastes every time he reads the poem). Psychoanalytic lore tells me that the sensations of being hot and sweaty might also play a part in a fantasy built on the earliest stage of infancy when the skin was unusually sensitive to being too hot or too cold, too wet or too dry. This, however, would seem farfetched to me, if I did not feel that they therefore related to a "Lady" who whispers a song as though her breathing took over everyone else's. Feel-ings of merger, identity, time, and waiting would also fit in this context. But I must quickly admit that these psycho-analytic observations gave me only the beginnings of a co-herence for the poem.

I find myself drawn to the theme of time. The title con-tains the word "day" in the form of a reversal of "Lady Day," as Billie Holiday was called; and then right after the title, the word occurs three times: "a Friday / three days after Bastille day." Then the poem states its year, 1959 (in digits) and, in that same first stanza, three times, all stated right down to the minute, also in digits, 12:20, 4:19, and 7:15, which seem to me to insist on a preciseness I have trouble associating with the Long Island Rail Road.

I get a most intense feeling of moments as moments. O'Hara will go "straight to dinner." He will read what poets in Ghana are doing "these days" or buy Behan's "new play" or two recent plays by Genet. Finally he does buy that day's paper. Then comes, for me, the crucial line, yet so casual, so elliptical, so thrown away, that I still find myself filling in the logic of it: her "face" on the paper means her picture means the news of her death. For me, that is *the* great moment in the poem. I feel as though I have unexpectedly stepped off a

curb into space and my heart suddenly tightens as I begin to
fall. The poem becomes very intense for me (her "face," not
her picture; "I am sweating a lot by now"). The last stanza
seems to me very fast, completely focused on the moment and
then, in the final phrase, slow and breathless, stopped after
each word despite the grammatical slide through a doubly
functioning "everyone"—"to Mal Waldron and everyone and
I stopped breathing."

The time I am responding to, then, is not simply time but
moments, particularly moments which go away or come back,
which fade or persist. Similarly, the poem's curious dating of
itself with reference to Bastille Day reminds me that the Bastille
itself is gone, but the day endures (and my pun makes sense
in the poem). Similarly, "Hesiod" refers, no doubt, to his
Works and Days, and I am also struck by the contrast between
the permanence of Hesiod and the skillful but temporary translations of Richmond Lattimore, here rendered by what the
eye instantaneously sees, the abbreviation "trans." Banks are
about as permanent as modern society gets, but presumably
O'Hara's balance ebbs and flows as mine does. The teller "for
once in her life" does not look it up—he "once heard" her
name, which itself comprises both movement and nonmove-
ment: "Stillwagon." This is a poem of momentary, casual,
strolling impulses—and against them the sudden shock of that
last moment recalled.

The names give part of the feeling of casualness in the
poem: Patsy, Mike, Mal Waldron—I'm not at all sure who
they are. Although, as it happens, I know the places, others
may not: Easthampton, the Ziegfeld Theatre, the stores around
58th Street and Sixth Avenue, the 5 Spot. Contrasted to all
these, "she" is never named, except by allusion in the title. As
against that bright, hot, summer street "she" is in a dark,
smoky, crowded nightclub, so intimate and so close it is as if
she breathed for me.

From names like "5 Spot" one can educe another theme. As one of my students pointed out—I had not noticed them—the names introduce all kinds of foreign things: the Bastille, Ghana, Verlaine, Bonnard, Hesiod, Brendan Behan, Genet, Strega, and Gauloises. These words describe sensuous or esthetic experiences, weakness, quandary, exoticism, even *préciosité*, while other words which have a distinctly American quality—"hamburger," "malted," "shoeshine," the *New York Post*, "6th Avenue," "john door"—relate to food or to the lady. To me, this contrast implies she is so known, so native, she need never be named, and thus they fill out the theme I have come to feel dominant in the poem: reversal.

The great reversal is the shock at the end of the fourth stanza when the poet sees Billie Holiday's picture in the *Post* and learns she has died. Suddenly light becomes dark, outside turns to inside, the foreign gives way to the native, sights and tastes yield to sounds. Most important, a series of casual, trivial moments become one that is heavy and portentous and, in a way, timeless, when separateness becomes a room in which everyone, spellbound, stops breathing (as the dead singer did on that July 17, 1959).

Thus the form I find in this poem is a complicated reversal of time and dependencies, signaled by details like the ritual transformations in the two plays of Genet he mentions or, more centrally, the change in the title of Lady Day to Day Lady. At first, in this poem, O'Hara seems dependent, someone who is being fed by strangers, but as the poem proceeds he becomes the nurturer of his friends Patsy and Mike. Then in the last lines of the poem, he seems to sustain Billie Holiday as she sustained him. He has her great art (and his) hold a moment frozen for all time, while at an unconscious level, I, at least, fantasy a return to an at-oneness with an all-powerful Lady, also felt as forever.

His momentary fusion with her whispered breathing involves me forever with the ephemera of his day, July 17, 1959. It gives him and his friends whom I do not know a name and habitation in my mind, because I care about Billie Holiday. Her art, the most fleeting of all, the improvising, the singing, the very breathing, of jazz makes their fugitive identities and O'Hara's ephemeral lunch hour forever permanent. Yet it is his art, the lyric poet's traditional and magical power to create immortality by his elegies, which makes her evanescent art forever permanent. The poem works for me a reversal in this larger sense: it builds out of the poet's impermanences and the Lady's impermanences, a paradoxical "day" of immortality. Each impermanence makes the other immortal to create one of the most astonishing elegies of our time. Its very transiency ensures the immortality of both Lady and poem. The momentary act of living and writing the poem becomes part of the poem's mourning for all momentary things, and the poem becomes part of the long tradition of the elegy in English precisely because it insists on its freedom from that tradition, its complete instantaneity.

As I edge over into the conventions of formal criticism, though, it is well to remember that it is not the poem which does these things but the way I re-create the poem for myself and for you who read me. I have moved from a frank account of my feelings to the application of outside knowledge, then to the language of formal explication which follows the less-than-candid convention that what I attribute to the poem is "in the poem." In fact, what I have done is complete and protect my feelings about the poem through the analysis of it I have given. I have rationalized my pleasure—indeed, added to it by making sense of a sequence of images that seemed to me insultingly random, a mastery that succeeds only because it is logical and coherent to me.

Naturally, I hope you share my reading, but I know that you may not, although I have tried to be as objectively logical and convincing as I could. I had to, to succeed in mastering the randomness of this "action" poem to my own satisfaction. I can now justify to myself the presence of every image and word in the poem, even to the "yes" in the second line. (It settles a momentary uncertainty as to what year it is and noticing how long a year is compared to that brief uncertainty, gives me again a theme of time and transiency and the reversal of the instantaneous toward the timeless.) I have introduced a psychoanalytic concept of orality, but for the most part I have relied on simple groupings or contrasts among images which are undeniably "there." Inevitably, I have introduced some subjective colorings, my recollections of that part of Manhattan or the taste of Gauloises or the sound of Billie Holiday; my assumption that the 5 Spot is dark; my association of ritual transformation with the plays of Genet; most crucially, my feeling that the final, breathless scene has weight and moment and importance. I don't see how this much subjectivity could be avoided or why it should be.

My reading combines, then, very personal feelings and intuitions toward the poem with more logical and objective analysis. Whether *I* accept my reading depends a great deal on that logic, objectivity, and precision, because I am that kind of person. But your acceptance depends very little on those things. If the intuitions feel right, you will supply the evidence for them yourself.

Whether the intuitions feel right depends on whether you can share, at least partly, my re-creation and synthesis of the poem. Specifically, can you use the defense and adaptation expressed in my personal transformation of the poem as I have told it to you? You need only accept a part—for example, the contrast between what is foreign and what is native and original. You may find the reversal of the momentary into the eternal a congenial theme, or the named unknowns into the unnamed knowns, or the light into the dark, or the random

into the orally organized. Only you can say, for only if you
find my reading consolidates and supports the integrity of
your own can you share my view of the poem. Logic and precision on my part may help you to use my interpretation—or
they may interfere—but they are not crucial. It is by re-
creating part of your ego style from part of mine as I have expressed it in my reading of the poem that you bestow your
acceptance.

If you make my reading part of your synthesis of the
poem, you do so in a quite specific way. You take things I
said to construct your particular adaptive pattern. You use
statements of mine just as you use parts of the poem. *Vis-à-vis*
the reader, the critic and teacher of literature stands alongside
the writer. His statements serve the reader as the writer's do,
although they cannot, of course, claim the same authority.
That is, one can believe or disbelieve or simply ignore what a
critic says, since he makes statements of fact or opinion about
the work. The poet cannot be disbelieved, for, in Sidney's fine
phrasing, "he nothing affirmeth, and therefore never lieth."
From the reader's point of view, both what the poet says *and*
what the critic asserts provide him with raw materials for his
personal re-creation of the poem. In our analogy, the poet is
like the builder of the classic temple, and the critic is a later
Roman improver. *Both* provide foundations and walls for a
mosque which both was and was not the original temple and
which neither the original architect nor his Roman redecorator
could have imagined.

We have seen critical commentary fail when I brusquely
explicated a couple of lines from "There is a spell," trying to
get Saul to respond. He simply remained silent, finally saying
he had "no reaction." It also failed when I urged Sandra to
think about "There is a spell" as "a poem about the creation
of the poem itself, in other words, the poem being the pearl of
great price."

Yeah, but I still don't understand. . . . What's the shell, really you know? Is that the traditional way that you would cut yourself off from whatever is outside? Because a poet can't do that really for very long.

My reading could not work for her because it did not help her absorb the poem's ending into her character structure. She felt it had "negative overtones," was "kind of a bitter thing, I suppose," because it stopped the exchange and mutual filling she hoped for from other beings.

Once a reader has synthesized a poem for himself, one can see in quite specific detail what parts he used and how he used them, both to ward off anxiety and to achieve pleasure, as you and I have seen Saul and Sandra and Seymour do. Equally, one can see how a reader did or did not take over and use part or all of the way someone else constructed the poem, as you have seen Saul and Sandra reject my interpretations or yourself accept (I hope) Seymour's reading of "The Day Lady Died."

These understandings show that the literary transaction is highly fluid with no fixed boundaries or outcomes, indeed, practically nothing fixed except the words on the page and the characteristic patterns a reader brings to them. One cannot predict what he will say or do, although one can understand it quite exactly in retrospect. Nor can I say in any simple way that some other reader's synthesis is wrong, even though I cannot accept it myself. For example, someone has suggested to me that "The Day Lady Died" deals with the idea that in the modern, urban world which is the ambience of this poem, the death, even of a person as admired and persecuted as Billie Holiday, becomes as trivial as any other momentary event. Someone else reads the poem as saying that, in the face of death, which stops finally the flow of time, place, and event, the most minute details of life take on immense importance. Both these readings make sense—that is, they do not involve obvious misstatements of fact about the poem. I can't "prove" them wrong, but still they do not fit what I need to feel about "The Day Lady Died," and I cannot therefore believe them, not without some further explanation, anyway, by which I could absorb them into my personal synthesis of the poem.

IV

The psychoanalytic model of the literary experience explains not only the bond between reader and work but also the way others' comments do or do not enter into that first, private relation. It therefore describes the inner dynamics of that most familiar situation in which people affect the degree and manner in which other people achieve literary works for themselves—the curious collectivity into which the individuals assembled in a theater merge.

To each individual, the general principle that describes the one-to-one relation applies: he uses the play or film as a resource from which to build up his characteristic ego style. He tries to match his defensive and adaptive patterns with some exactitude so he can very freely admit his fantasies. The second rule states that others' comments and reactions to the work can also provide raw material for a personal synthesis. In a theater, to the physical play or film in front of the individual member of the audience, are added the reactions of those around him, at least to the extent those reactions are visible: "They are laughing." "They are moved." "They are restless." "They think this is awful." Each member of the audience perceives these at the very moment he perceives the dramatic work itself. They weigh powerfully into the balance of his adaptations because they enter at precisely the touchiest point—the synthesis of defenses.

If the individual member of the audience disagrees with the people around him (for example, if he laughs when they are moved or if he tries to shush them because he is moved and they are laughing), then to the threats with which his defenses must deal, he adds the loss of esteem from his neighbors. Conversely, if he agrees with them, he eases his task of adaptation by subtracting these potential threats from the real or imagined dangers he has to deal with. These peer opinions involve a surprisingly grave threat. Many experiments have shown that a group opinion will make an individual change even such black-and-white factual statements as the relative length of two lines.[4] If the audience around him rejects the work, and if the individual accepts that rejection, he makes the work unavailable to himself for synthesizing his defenses. Conversely, if the audience reacts positively and the individual agrees, the work becomes that much more available to him.

The presence of an active (laughing, sighing, fidgeting, weeping) audience, as distinct from a mere critical reputation, thus exerts a doubly powerful pressure on disparate individuals toward a consensus, and it presses on the literary synthesis at precisely the most delicate point. Producers and directors have sensed this state of affairs for centuries and hired claques and catcallers and "canned" laughter accordingly, but the concept of an identity theme and ego style explains psychologically how the collectivity of the audience works on the inner dynamics of individual response.

Something of the same pressure generates the need most people feel to have others agree with their interpretation or evaluation of a work. When as a critic I construct a theory of "The Day Lady Died," it serves a number of purposes for me. In particular, it justifies and protects my own felt response by an appeal to higher ego functions such as logic, literary experience, skill at thematics, or sensitivity to words. I use those abilities to consolidate and integrate my fragmentary, intuitive impulse toward the poem into a total experience of gratification and cohesion (within the four principles we have seen). As in a theater, others, by accepting or rejecting my theory of the work, can make it more or less of a justification of my own response. Hence I (and, I think, every critic) feel a need to persuade others to use my or his theory of the work to consolidate their own responses. Often, feeling this need, the critic will claim his reading is "objective" or "authoritative." In fact, all that claim really amounts to is the critic's assertion that others can *share* his private synthesis, using a communal acceptance to achieve personal mastery for themselves—and for the critic.

This psychoanalytic model describes the particulars of another situation in which one person affects the degree and manner with which someone else achieves a literary work for himself—the teaching of literature. At the most immediate level, a teacher affects his students' experience by giving them greater resources with which to form the work for themselves. For example, a teacher may simply convey information: it takes some knowledge of Chaucer's Middle English or Milton's theology or Shakespeare's bawdy to experience their works fully. A teacher may also try to teach skills, ways of synthesizing literature for oneself in a general way, such as assessing tone, putting characters together, or finding unities. All these, the student will assimilate to the extent he can make them serve the basic strategies of his character.

The teacher intervenes in a more problematical way when he becomes involved in interpretations or, more generally, commentary. Teaching literature, as we know it today, is a misnomer. One cannot teach literature itself; one can only teach students to make statements about literature. Similarly, criticism is not the experience of literature or art as such, but the taking of positions about them. Not so long ago, the teaching of literature favored only statements based in the periods and categories of literary history, while criticism consisted of the critic's narrating "the adventures of his soul among masterpieces" (in Anatole France's phrase). With the coming of "new" or formalist criticism in the 1930s and 1940s, both teaching and criticism in America and England turned toward statements of the inner coherence and intricacy of the work (beauties necessarily in the eye of the beholder but, by convention, attributed to the beheld). One of the most refreshing of recent trends in teaching and criticism (both in America and abroad) has been the opening up of literature to many other types of statement: dicta from anthropology, mythology, psychology, philosophy, or structuralism.

Even so, teaching literature by applying other disciplines to texts (indeed, by any commentary) faces an inherent limitation—namely, that it is just that, commentary. It affects someone's inner experience of literature indirectly, only to the extent he can use it to pass the literary work through his defensive and adaptive boundaries. It does not work directly with those boundaries and it therefore represents a hit-or-miss approach subject to the inherent personal qualities of each student and also to changes in intellectual fashion. For example, in the United States, with the passing of the button-down collar and the narrow tie of the Kennedy era, we have seen students become less and less able to use the tight, close textual analyses of the "new" critics for their own syntheses of literary works. Boundaries loosened in the late sixties, and students call for freer approaches to literature.

For this and many other reasons, teachers would like to teach—or at least remove obstacles to—the experience itself. For example, one occasionally finds students who resist literary experiences because they feel they are somehow effeminate. From a psychological point of view, this resistance to poetry typically expresses a deeper resistance to one's own passive needs, feared because they imply an unmanning, being made a woman. Our model suggests that the way to deal with such a resistance to literature is to get these feelings out in the open.

Why is poetry thought of as feminine? How and why does our culture link passivity to femininity? Do all cultures? Surely there are moments, in sports, for example, or sex, when a man, precisely by relaxing his controls and giving himself to the experience, is most manly. As a psychoanalytic aphorism has it, to be truly a man, one must accept the woman in oneself.

The same freeing applies to questions less obviously psychological, seemingly more literary. For example, there are always students who object to the stylized and allusive locutions of the English eighteenth-century poets or (a more serious loss) the great French dramatists of the seventeenth century. Stylization gives up detail in the present to replace it by allusions to a historical or mythological past or some other more general system of thought (so I see it, anyway). If so, then one must ask someone who does not like the poetry of allusion and stylization why he feels immediate detail ("my Pound thing" as Saul said) more satisfactory than appeals to generality. How do details feel to him? What—and one would have to arrive at this by indirection—what function do details serve in his psychic economy?

Another familiar objection is to sentimentality or, as it is usually put, to characters who are too good (or too evil) to be believable. Again, the literary complaint mingles with a psychological rejection. Some readers may feel that a writer like Goldsmith or Dickens glosses over sex or aggression that feels, somehow, more intensely real. Why does it feel especially real? Why would someone want it to be expressed by a writer and not hidden? Other readers may object to the interpretation of reality through morals-colored glasses. Again, one senses deeper, more personal issues about feeling the acceptance of parental and social values as a caving in.

In general, a teacher comes to understand his students' literary objections (or a critic his readers' resistances) by listening for the difficulties they are meeting in matching their defensive patterns. And to gain this greater closeness to students' and readers' responses, one must allow discussions which are ostensibly literary to range far afield and deep within. This is an inevitable corollary of the principle that poems exist for and in persons, not vice versa.

Even this kind of teaching or criticism, though, attempts only the removal of obstacles. There can be a more positive approach, one which tries directly to teach people to have a literary experience. The model (that is, the four principles of interaction plus the idea of the literary experience as a transformation) suggests that such teaching has to proceed in two directions. In one, the discussion draws closer to the text, bringing to bear whatever skills and knowledge open the text to the students, particularly by a resonance of person to person. With the O'Hara poem, one asks, for example, what kind of person says, "I don't know the people who will feed me," or "practically [goes] to sleep with quandariness." One might conclude that the randomness in the poem expresses a deeper passivity which was precisely what enabled O'Hara to re-create Billie Holiday in just the breathtaking way he did.

At the same time, the discussion has to move in the opposite direction, away from the text and through the ways different readers give it life toward at least a tentative sense of the readers' own identity themes and their interactions with the text and one another. Obviously, this requires tact and discretion, the very opposite of the familiar kind of slambang symbol-twirling or shot-from-the-hip diagnoses that people commonly associate with psychoanalytic criticism. I have found that if you safeguard privacy and steer the discussion away from intimacies and confessions, even relatively inexperienced readers can become alert to their emotions and associations as they read. Within a positive and encouraging discussion, students soon begin to articulate their feelings, making them more available to themselves and others. Typically, a student then be-

gins to have both more feelings and more of a literary experience, if for no other reason than sheer curiosity about himself.

In such a learning context, a reader uses the fine, subtle
listening "new" critics have taught these last decades to
listen to himself and to others with the same attention to detail
and nuance that formerly was reserved for literature as a separate entity. Conversely, he can try to talk about feelings and
associations with as much precision as a good formalist critic
brings to his verbal analyses. In learning more about himself,
he learns more about literature, as in learning more about literature, he learns more of his own inner dynamics. But this mutuality comes about only in a setting where it is taken for
granted that literature is a human experience and to be studied
as such, not in formal or historical isolation.

I do not, however, mean to suggest in the slightest sense
that classes in literature should become encounter groups or
therapy sessions. Few literary people have the temperamental
wish to change the psychic functioning of another. Still fewer,
I think, will find they have the "helping" frame of mind so
essential to the physician or therapist—and *chutzpah* is no substitute for it. I do insist, however, on literature as a human
experience and reality. So understood, it need not be a private
sanctum where mandarins and scholiasts generate statements
about statements about statements about literature, abstractions
piled upon terminologies leaning on metaphors based on dicta
precariously held up by still other abstractions. The foundation
and *Grundwahrheit* of teaching and criticism as human interactions is the human experience of art—it is toward this the
psychoanalytic model turns us, and neither to therapy nor to
pedantry.

V

To systematize the human experience of art, one must
have a viable psychology of human experience. Despite the

scientific claims of other psychologies, I have found them tantalizingly inconclusive, at least as applied to literature. Hence I have turned and returned to psychoanalytic psychology despite the prejudices and misinterpretations it evokes. Modern psychoanalysis offers the only psychology I know that can explain the choices of particular words which are, after all, the *Stoff* which I as a literary critic seek out, as well as a particularly important type of human behavior. At the same time, psychoanalysis provides at least some insights into the larger aspects of human experience: learning, politics, the arts, religion, sex, science, love, youth, age, and all the things that make our lives lively. Until some other psychology offers such an extraordinary range from the particular to the general, I do not see how the literary critic has any other choice.

Having once decided on psychoanalysis or even another psychology, there are, in principle, two ways one brings it to bear on literature: as a specialized body of external knowledge and for a deeper mode of understanding one's own inner dynamics and those of others. In the first mode, one can apply psychoanalysis to a literary work as one can apply any body of theory, Marxist, Maoist, Christian, existential, structural, or astrological. And the literary work will yield illustrations, respectively, of psychoanalysis, Marxism, Maoism, Christianity, existentialism, structuralism, astrology, or any other theory brought to it to be illustrated. One can apply these theories jerkily and harshly or subtly and with gentleness, but either way, I find I usually feel dissatisfied. If one does nothing more than prove that such-and-such a literary work illustrates the principles of class warfare, the theories of some French *savant*, the antics of a digital computer, or even the psychoanalytic insights I admire and enjoy, I feel cheated. The work has been reduced and schematized in a game of "Heads I win, tails you lose."

One can do better, however, if one does not settle simply

for cranking the work through a formula but uses a body of specialized knowledge like psychoanalytic psychology as a way into the encounter. For me, that means using it, for example, to discover relationships between seemingly unrelated parts of the work. One can also discover the ways in which the text represents a transformation of fantasy materials by means of adaptive and defensive strategies for the writer or for the reader. And, too, one can find some of the less obvious connections between the work and particular details and events in the author's life.

For an example, we can use one long established psycho-analytic generalization. People for whom "taking in" acts as a major source of pleasure are likely to have established this modality during earliest infancy. "Taking in" in this context may well have meanings derived from food, taste, and the mouth. At later stages of development, such people are likely to relate to others by way of identification—taking them in or fusing or merging with them. "From the various methods of solution which are possible in the same diversified problem situations, the method represented by identification will be chosen preponderantly by persons in whom exist strong oral drives." [5]

Consider, in the light of this purely psychological item, perhaps the most startling (albeit nonpoetic) example of an eating fantasy in English literature: Swift's "A Modest Proposal for Preventing the Children of Ireland from Being a Burden to Their Parents or Country" (1729). Swift translated the political agony of Ireland into body terms: the mother country is eating her colony up; Irish babies should be raised like cattle and slaughtered for food. Consciously or unconsciously (one cannot tell, of course), Swift was working with a common fantasy: a hunger for food or nurture or mother that becomes ultimately the wish to eat mother herself and coupled with it the fear that she, out of love or retaliation, will eat you.

It survives in the similar nightmares of ferocious animals or monsters, and it shows its closeness to infantile love in such terms of endearment as "Sweetie" or "Honey" or in remarks to children like, "You're so cute, I could eat you up."

Psychoanalytic insight suggests that there is a deep, body logic that links orality to identification; that therefore one might bring in the idea of identification to unify Swift's essay. Certainly one familiar form identification took for Swift and his readers was the Christian ceremony of the Eucharist: identification—incorporation, really—of Christian charity by eating Christ. Eating Irish babies "would greatly lessen the number of Papists," says Swift, and he suggests the food would be particularly appropriate for taverns (perhaps recalling the flesh and wine of Christ's body or the birth of the Christ-child). He recalls a Formosan girl crucified and eaten. Swift's satire really attacks the failure to identify, however, as shown in the extraordinary deadpan tone of his numerical calculations of the feasibility of murder like the planner of an extermination camp. His speaker is as distant from his victims as a modern bombardier. To regard another human being as so-and-so many pounds of flesh, to dehumanize him totally, this complete de-identification is what Swift attacks.

Yet the opposite, total merger, is no better; it is, in a sense, just another way of dehumanizing people. In growing up, I (and, I am sure, you) developed a revulsion against expressing love simply and directly by eating the loved one up. The desire became reversed into its opposite, disgust. This reversal, which a psychoanalyst would call a "reaction-formation," corresponds exactly to the *reductio ad absurdum* method of Swift's satire. He suggests that I eat babies, and I react to this apparently serious suggestion with disgust and horror, so much so that I become quite generally disgusted with such "scientific" projects, disgusted at the way England fed on the Irish, disgusted at man's inhumanity to man, and I cast about in my

mind for better ways of identifying with the Irish than eating
them. Interestingly, in one paragraph Swift lists some alternatives to his scheme, but they all take the form of anti-identifica-
tion, of setting oneself off, alone and apart. The Irish are to
trade only within their country, cease their internal struggles,
and firm up a close, inward, national identity, isolated from all
foreign influences, another kind of distance and identification.

In short, the purely psychological observation about orality permits me to find an underlying logic and unity between
Swift's bizarre food scheme, the scientific tone with which he
presents it, and the real remedies he obliquely states. Obviously,
other information about orality applies to other literary works.
For example, psychiatrists have long known there is a close
link between the extremes of mania and depression and early
feeding experiences. Similarly, people who approach the world
as if they were going to be fed by it often perceive experiences
in all-or-nothing terms. You can sample these feelings for yourself by imagining the state of the infant: the feeding mother is
either wholly there or utterly absent; he is either being totally
gratified or he is completely frustrated and despairing.[6]

In the light of these clinical observations, see how Keats
uses images of taste in these well-known lines from the great
"Ode on Melancholy":

Ay, in the very temple of delight
    Veil'd Melancholy has her sovran shrine,
        Though seen of none save him whose strenuous tongue
    Can burst Joy's grape against his palate fine;
His soul shall taste the sadness of her might,
        And be among her cloudy trophies hung.

I can understand Keats's portrait of joy and melancholy in the
light of a psychological generalization: that it is precisely the
man who can feel joy most ecstatically who will be most subject to depression. The insight from the study of mind enables

me to find a rich inner coherence in Keats's use of images of taste and the mouth to realize his feeling of merger and being overwhelmed by the maternal might of melancholy.

The psychological observation gives a special dimension to these linked themes of having all or nothing, total depression or total elation, that to taste joy is to risk being engulfed by melancholy—alternatively, that not to have all is to have nothing, as in the late sonnet, "To Fanny":

I cry your mercy—pity—love!—aye, love!
    Merciful love, that tantalizes not,
One-thoughted, never-wandering, guileless love,
    Unmask'd, and being seen—without a blot!
O! let me have thee whole,—all—all—be mine!
    That shape, that fairness, that sweet minor zest
Of love, your kiss,—those hands, those eyes divine,
    That warm, white, lucent, million-pleasured breast,—
Yourself—your soul—in pity give me all,
    Withhold no atom's atom or I die,
Or living on perhaps, your wretched thrall,
    Forget, in the mist of idle misery,
Life's purposes,—the palate of my mind
Losing its gust, and my ambition blind! *

---

* Merely as a parenthesis, now that we are drawing near the end of this book, you may be curious to know why I have built so much of it around this one type of fantasy, the oral. Obviously, I have reasons for doing so which stem from my own personality structure, and you know enough about me at this point to infer at least some of them. At a more intellectual level, this particular fantasy fits this book because of some other choices: writing about H.D.; describing the sense of being "absorbed" in literature; the wish to mobilize as little resistance as possible. But there is a third reason. Long ago, I was stung by a comment on psychoanalytic criticism made by a man both intelligent and sympathetic to psychoanalysis:

The obvious limitation of traditional Freudian literary analysis is that only one study can be written, since every additional one would turn out to say the same thing. Ernest Jones could do a beautiful job

Again, images of flavor and the mouth pervade, this time a poem of craving and hunger. The first quatrain demands complete commitment to the lover, which if granted equals total unity, no duality at all—again, one either has everything, as in the first quatrain, or nothing, as in the last four lines. Keats may even have chosen the word "atom" for its original meaning of "indivisible." The reference to the breast fits the psychological pattern, as does the very Keatsian phrasing, "million-pleasured breast," which does not locate the pleasure either in the lover or the breast alone, as "mouth" or "blushful" in the "Ode to a Nightingale" do not distinguish the drinker from what is drunk:

> O for a beaker full of the warm South,
>   Full of the true, the blushful Hippocrene,
>   With beaded bubbles winking at the brim,
>   And purple-stained mouth.

These lines suggest the ease of Keats's mergers and identifications, while the sonnet moves from the ecstasy of total possession and fusion to the depression of total loss in its final images, which describe an end to "taking in" through mouth or eye.

Knowledge of psychological links like that between feeding and depression will enable a reader to find unexpected unities in literary works themselves. It will also let him see the

---

finding the underlying Oedipus complex in *Hamlet,* but had he gone on to analyze *Lear* or *A Midsummer Night's Dream* or the *Sonnets* he would have found to his surprise that they reflected Shakespeare's Oedipus complex too, and, in fact, granting his theories, he would have made the same discovery about any other work of art. A criticism that can only say, however ingeniously, that this work is a result of the author's repressed Oedipal desires, turns out not to be saying very much.

Troubled by the misunderstandings this paragraph revealed, I resolved someday to write a book about psychoanalytic criticism in which the oedipus complex did not appear at all. This is it, and I have very nearly succeeded.

unity between the writer and his writings. At a simple, almost trivial level, by recognizing the strongly oral coloration of Keats's personality and his use of identification as a defensive form in his poems, you can see the importance in his life of such details as his sensitivity about what he thought was his overly large mouth, his fondness for "concerts" in which he and his friends would mouth the sounds of the various instruments (Keats liked to be the bassoon), his tendency to depend on older friends, his search for an identity by systematically setting out to "be a Poet," or his identification with a series of earlier or older poetic models. You can see, too, the significance in Keats's total style of such a literary crux as the ending of *Endymion:* to have achieved a compromise, an imperfect part, like the Indian Maid, is an unstable position; she must become either nothing or all—the unattainable moon goddess.

Keats's dominant psychological pattern is one of identification. By tasting a small satisfaction—or a small sorrow—taking it into himself, he becomes able to identify with, really to lose himself in, a total, all-encompassing reality. Knowing this, one can see the organic relation between biographical data (the deaths in Keats's family, for example) and his large themes, such as his famous characterization (in images of taste) of the "camelion Poet" and the poetical character: "It does no harm from its relish of the dark side of things any more than from its taste for the bright one; because they both end in speculation." Identification also sustains his great conception of the sympathetic imagination as something that would let him imagine himself into a billiard ball and feel its "sense of delight from its own roundness, smoothness and [the] very volubility . . . of its motion." From the same psychological point of view, you can see the organic relations between his tendency to link in his poems sleep and poetry or the imagination and trance, his recurring wishes "To cease upon the midnight," to "drink, and leave the world unseen, / And with thee fade away," and his extraordinary ability to think himself into small tactile details while reaching always for the total, the ineffable, and the transcendent.

One can, in short, hold up psychoanalytic psychology like any other body of external knowledge beside a literary work and so discover unities within the work. With psychoanalysis, however, one also finds unities between the work and its author and among the conscious moral and intellectual themes, the unconscious and infantile fantasy content, and the forms by which one becomes the other. All these are apparently "in" the work, which can be treated as an external reality to be studied by external knowledge. Yet the very psychology we apply tells us that these things are not "in" the work at all but in our interaction with the work.

Using psychoanalysis as external knowledge can turn it into a rigid scheme of rules and symbols; certainly the earliest applications of psychoanalysis to literature did just that. They converted psychoanalysis into, in Erikson's term, an "originology," which decoded manifest behavior into its source, either events in infancy or illnesses in the adult. Works of art often served primarily as clues to the writer's childhood, neuroses, or sexual idiosyncrasies, in the esthetic studies by the old masters of psychoanalysis, sometimes even by Freud himself. Today one would recognize that this kind of reading backward from the adult to the child or the neurotic tells only half the story. It is at least as important to see the forward move: the way the creative human being transforms the nubs and knots of early life into later achievements which fulfill the needs of inner and outer reality for the adult. A modern view would see the human being as playing infinite variations upon a continuing, central identity theme, as we have done.

The very psychoanalysis, then, that reveals these unities tells us that psychoanalysis cannot be applied simply as external knowledge the way a political, economic, or esthetic theory can. Because it shows that people take in experiences by building up from them their structure of defenses and adaptations, it shows how people create psychoanalysis for themselves too. Modern psychoanalysis must serve, not as a fixed system of rules and symbols, but as a way of becoming aware of one's own characteristic reactions to all kinds of "others," other experiences, external systems of knowledge, other people, and literary works. I am the sensing instrument for understanding the experiences I have.

At first glance, this would seem to put us into an infinite regress. Sandra (through her identity theme) perceives H.D.'s poem. I (through my identity theme) perceive Sandra perceiving (through her identity theme) H.D.'s poem. As you read this book, you perceive (through your identity theme) my perceiving (through my identity theme) Sandra perceiving (through her identity theme) H.D.'s poem. And so on. Looked at narrowly, we seem to have bogged down in a morass of subjectivity. From a larger perspective, however, while individual perceptions follow individual character structures, the general law applies generally. It tells us that people take in the "other" by building up from it their structure of defense and adaptation. The physical reality of the other, be it literary text or the real world or what someone else says, serves as building blocks. The blocks take their shape, color, and other properties from their source, but it is the person who builds with the blocks who determines the structure that results, much like our Christian or Turkish architects.

In short, we began with literary questions, but we end with a general law of human psychology—and even as I write that, I realize that I have thereby fulfilled my own characteristic tendency to generalize, to find geometry in a seashell. Before opening up that large principle, I think I can best free the ideas of this book for *your* characteristic reconstruction of them by retracing the steps and summarizing the specific inquiries by which I brought us to this general question.

VI

We began with a writer, a very special writer, Hilda Doolittle. Her account of her analysis with Freud showed her personality developing and working itself out through the various stages of her childhood, in her relations with mother, father, brothers, and analyst, and in her mystical visions and mythologies. I interpreted her lifestyle as representing a great many variations on a central, early theme: "to close the gap with signs." Then one could see, in her poetry, the same identity theme worked out and varied in her two major literary styles, first Imagism, then a richly symbolic and mythological mode. The content of her poems accented the drives in her personality, toward nurture, mastery, and a fusion with masculine hardness. The forms, the exact rendering of images, the short stanzas, or the mythological references expressed more the defensive side of her ego style, while her themes, the sense of reality as a palimpsest, for example, or her preoccupation with the battle of the sexes had more to do with the adaptive aspect of her personal myth. But these are distinctions of degree only.

The essential thing was to recognize the human organism as indeed organic: H.D. as having a unitary, centering principle from which she created infinite variations and capabilities. Just as it is difficult in literature to isolate form from content from theme from style, so in life, to speak of drives or defenses or adaptations or autonomous ego functions or object relations or neuroses—almost any of the traditional psychoanalytic categories—is simply to accent one aspect or another of that central identity theme or one particular group of its transformations. As applied to a writer, this way of understanding someone through his identity theme and its variations will show how the fact of his writing and even the very type and style of it fulfills the basic law of his being. Inevitably, a writer, in creating a literary work, achieves a multiple solution to the demands of his inner and outer reality, a variation on his identity theme. I can, therefore, understand both his life-style and his literary style, creative living and creative writing, by the same principles of transformation and variation.

When what the writer has created reaches a reader, how-ever, the reader perceives it, not in terms of the writer's iden-tity theme but his own. Although I could not offer you the wealth of information about Saul and Sandra (and Seymour) that we had for H.D., nevertheless you saw that they re-sponded to H.D.'s poem in terms of the same identity theme with which they created stories for their TAT tests. Just as one lives by creating variations of an identity theme, so one takes in experience through it, and this led to the overarching principle which governs the way readers re-create literary works for themselves. *Style seeks itself.* Each reader tries to compose from the elements of the work a match to his own characteristic style.

Three more principles set out this relation in more detail. Crucial to the reader's synthesis is the first, his matching his defenses in the text: only to the extent he can shape the materials of the text into his characteristic patterns of defense or adaptation does he really admit elements of the work into his mental functioning. Second, once he has admitted them, he uses the elements he has taken in to create a fantasy of the type that matters to him. Third, by means of the defenses he has matched, he transforms that fantasy toward a moral, esthetic, or intellectual "point" that enables him to find in the work unity, significance, and pleasure.

Together, these four principles mean that the reader has made the work participate in his own characteristic transformations of his identity theme. He no longer feels a distinction between "in here" and "out there," between him and it. Indeed, there is none, and he becomes, as we say, "absorbed." He and the work (as he has synthesized it) blend and merge in a potential space between perceiver and perceived where distinctions between inside and outside, self and other, found object and created object, objective reality and created symbol, have ceased to matter.

At first glance, one would think the writer controls through the text the experience the reader has, but, if so, then the work of art would be a fixed stimulus eliciting a fixed response, and simple experience tells us that is not the case. The idea that the writer magically controls his reader is only a figure of speech—he cannot prevent readers from making the most dreadful hash of what he has written. Indeed, almost any book review of large circulation will contain at least one letter to the editor from an indignant writer who feels a reviewer has done just that.

Rather, the writer creates a structure which his reader re-creates for himself. He does so with more or less violence to the text. Sometimes a reader will omit or ignore parts, distort, squeeze meanings and conclusions out, posit farfetched connections, and so on. But the reader who commits none of these sins still has a great deal of flexibility. When the poem says "seashell" or "beaker" or "atom" or "Bastille day," the reader will flesh those words out with meanings that suit him, because, even at the level of simple dictionary interpretations, the poem does not offer referents, neither general concepts nor particular conceptions, only words.

Different readers can interpret the same text very differently and still remain within the range of "correctness." Think, for example, of the many journals and the huge conventions of critics and teachers, largely devoted to new readings of old works, all predicated on a marketplace of competing interpretations. Various people construct the same poem variously when they are being their most intellectual and professional, all the more when they are freely airing their emotions.

Many common experiences tell us that the artist, even the creator of a masterpiece, exercises no final control over response. To me, the Cathedral at Chartres is the most magnificent artistic achievement of the high Middle Ages—I find it a massive, overpowering experience. Yet the dedicated and mysterious artisans can never be said to control my secular and twentieth-century experience of their collective work. I cannot believe they would be pleased by my awe at the size of their encyclopedia when I do not include a belief in its contents, and they might be quite pained when I associate the labyrinth in the floor of the nave with ancient symbols for the persephonic Magna Mater.

If the artist does not control his audience's response, what does he do? Freud wondered about the way artists' fantasies please their audiences but other people's do not, and he concluded: "The essential *ars poetica* lies in the technique of overcoming the feeling of repulsion in us which is undoubtedly connected with the barriers that rise between each single ego and the others." [7] Just as the model of literature-as-transformation expands Freud's early analysis of jokes, so the four principles of response developed here fill out this early surmise of his.

The artist leaves behind him a structure he thinks complete, and so it is—for him. For his audience, however, it is an experience yet to be realized, and different people will realize it in different ways. Some will try to get out what the artist intended (despite the "intentional fallacy"). Others will pursue a "true" interpretation. Professional readers may try to set the work in an historical or biographical or theoretical framework. All, however, will try to build an experience from some or all of the words—the raw materials—the writer left behind him and within the constraints imposed by the ordinary syntactic and semantic relations among those words. The writer's magic rests in his ability to bring together words and constraints on words from which people can compose experiences with unity, diversity, and intensity—or whatever terms you feel describe literary value. The "feeling of repulsion" of which Freud spoke, the barrier between ego and ego, comes down because one ego builds its characteristic functioning out of creations which are characteristic functions of another ego.

Recognizing the reader's creative role in the literary trans-action readjusts many traditional ideas, but it does not imply that all readings of a poem have equal merit. True, all readers take over parts of a poem and assign them roles in their psychic economy, but any given reader may neglect part of the text, assign idiosyncratic meanings, and be inconsistent or arbitrary. Obviously, it is not true that anything anyone says about liter-ature is as good as what anyone else says. One can judge a reading by a variety of objective criteria: completeness, unity, accuracy, directness, and so on.

They do not exclude, however, an important subjective criterion. We would like to know if the reader has achieved a concept of the work which gave him a sense of personal mastery. Did he feel that he had achieved a unity, significance, and pleasure in the work? Then, can others share his reading? Will his personal concept and mastery of the work win the assent of a community of readers? It will be more likely to, presumably, if it meets our customary standards of logic, coherence, completeness, universality, and the rest of the "objective" criteria. But his reading can be as logical as Euclid, and others still will not be able to share it unless they can find in it a match to their own defensive and adaptive structures, their own ego style.

Thus I turned in the last chapter of this book from the private transaction between the artist and his work or the reader and the work to occasions where literature becomes an interpersonal experience, notably in audiences, teaching, and criticism. These are situations where one personality interacts with others, the writer with his readers, the teacher with a student, the critic with one of his readers, or one member of an audience with all the rest. We have shaded off from classical psychoanalysis, which is an individual, intrapsychic psychology, to some of the questions attempted in a group psychology. Here again, Freud has been ahead of us. We can generalize his explanations in *Group Psychology and the Analysis of the Ego* (1921) in these terms: because of needs and desires such as those for love, the individual lets the group conduct part of his psychological functioning for him. Freud emphasized the way group leaders would take on the role of fathers and therefore assume the functions of a superego (in Freud's thinking, the father incorporated as a permanent voice in the psyche). Today, with a larger concept of adaptation and the ego, one would see the relation between individual and group that Freud emphasized as one of a number of possibilities. Today, one would say that a person participates in the experience of others to the extent he can match from them the adaptations, defenses, and fantasies of his total lifestyle. The writer and the reader form a group, the teacher and the student, or the critic and his reader.

VII

In short, we have returned to the large psychological principle that has evolved from what began as a purely literary application of psychoanalysis. Because we agreed to look at literature in its natural habitat, people, we become involved in the interaction of the two: first, the creative writer with his creation; second, his reader with the same creation; and third, several readers as their readings interacted with one another. In each case, we saw the same principle apply. Apparently, it is a

basic pattern in human behavior to relate to the rest of the
human and nonhuman world by constructing from it one's characteristic pattern of adaptations through which one then projects and introjects wishes and fantasies, giving them a coherence by means of the adaptations one has synthesized. H.D.
created her poems and fictions by synthesizing her identity
theme from the experiences she had and the words that were
so essential to her to manage those experiences. Sandra and Saul
(and Seymour) read her work by creating their own ego
styles from it. Finally, I found that I could influence their
reading or yours, as critic and teacher, by adding to what the
poet gave, my own comments on the work—and these, too,
you would take in only to the extent you could compose your
own ego style from them. Whether or not you will be able to
accept this book, for example, will depend a great deal on
whether you can make out of my generalizing techniques and
my search for unities something that suits your own patterns
of defense. Finally, it appears that this personal mode of experiencing reality applies not just to literature and statements
about literature but to any interaction between a human being
and the world around him: he can take it in only to the extent
he can build up his own style from it.

The amoeba provides me (as it did Freud) a simple
analogy to this complex interaction. It reaches out its literal
pseudopods toward the world as we project our mental ones,
in search of things to take in. Some of what it surrounds can
pass through its barriers against physical and chemical invasion. What does pass from outside to inside becomes simply
part of the amoeba, much as experiences we take in become
part of us—that is, if they can match our defenses and so participate in our search for gratification. What cannot pass these
barriers does not enter the amoeba's protoplasm but remains
separate and is left behind as the amoeba continues to extend
itself into its environment. To the extent this simple proto-

zoon serves as the ancestor of more complex animals, to the
extent taking in food lays down the pattern for taking in
experience, the amoeba may be more than an analogy—an
evolutionary prototype.

Less speculative and closer to man are two concepts put
forward from child development by a group of English psychoanalytic theorists: the transitional object and potential
space. Both describe the way the young child bridges the gap
that opens between himself and his mother when he forms a
separate self (as we have seen in connection with H.D.'s
development and artistic "absorption"). The "security cloth"
is the most familiar transitional object, the warm, dirty piece of
blanket a child clutches and carries everywhere which substitutes for mother and yet is clearly perceived as not mother.
Any object can serve, however, so long as it has this property
of being both a thing and a symbol, both found and created
reality. Indeed, the English theorists would argue, after one
has acquired a sense of self, all important objects have this dual
reality. Similarly, the most sophisticated cultural experiences go
on in a space which is neither inner psychic reality nor external
reality (or, in the phrases I have been using, neither "in here"
nor "out there"). They go on in a "potential space" which
both joins and separates the individual and the person or thing
he cares about, which originally was the space between the
mother and the child separating a self from her.[8]

These concepts, drawn from child development studies,
depict, as does the amoeba, a creative organism actively seeking
and synthesizing its own relations with the world. As such,
they accord with some other strong themes in contemporary
psychological research, notably into perception and cognition.
Studies into perception show that animals and humans do not
simply see by letting light fall on a passive eye—rather they
need to test perceptions and generate changes and variations by
moving their limbs and themselves, or else distortions cannot

be corrected. Similarly, one learns to perceive verticality, horizontality, perspective, and other visual qualities by forming unconscious hypotheses about the meaning of converging lines, right-angle corners, and the like. Without these hypotheses, one cannot assemble stimuli into a coherent picture. Still more detailed studies show that the very eye movements used in vision follow out the individual's hypotheses about what he sees, which take the form of internal representations he holds up against the picture the experimenter offers him. Further, different individuals have different characteristic ways of forming these hypotheses and scanning the picture they are shown. In reading, in particular, we put letters together to form words by means of quick guesses from the first letters as to what the word is. When the text is scrambled to make such hypotheses impossible, reading becomes seriously slowed and impaired.[9]

In general, even in early infancy, the human seems to be a hypothesis-forming animal—indeed, recent experiments suggest that the child becomes able to form hypotheses about the same time that psychoanalytic observation finds self-object differentiation taking place, that is, between eight and twelve months of age. Jean Piaget's long and brilliant researches have shown the later evolution of the child's hypotheses about mass and energy and number and morality; and his concepts of assimilation (the organism's actively taking in from its environment) and accommodation (the environment's changing the organism's ways of taking in) match the complex interaction we have seen between the literary work and its re-creating reader. They fit, too, such a general view of the human being as George A. Kelly's personal construct theory: each man is a scientist, formulating constructs by which he anticipates events and interprets them. He then seeks out experiences to correct his constructs and make them as elaborate and powerful as possible. All such interactions place the person in what Gregory Bateson would call a "general system," his mind being part of a continuing process of generation and feedback in and with his surroundings.[10]

These theories and experiments insist that people are prehensile animals, actively reaching into their environment for experience. To this general view, psychoanalysis adds the psychoanalytic touch: understanding the organism's activity by taking consciousness as the primary datum and inferring from it unconscious forces in the present and from the past, both recent and remote, that shape the experiences sought and found. Psychoanalysis and these other trends that cut across the dualism of mind and body reveal the psychological dynamics within such philosophical concepts as John Dewey's "having an experience" or, still more apropos, the ingathering of here and there, subject and object, into that prehensive unification which is, according to Alfred North Whitehead, the organic reality humans know.

In other words, to return to the large problem with which this book began, "subjective" and "objective" are not so much predicates as words to describe two different stances from which to look at the process of experiencing. Necessarily I look at that process from inside me where all my experiences are subjective, that is, private and personal, and you can never know them. I build my experiences in part, however, from public realities which I perceive as outside both of us and which you can share with me. How you will experience those things, of course, I cannot know, but I suppose that you build your private experiences from them somewhat as I do mine. Further, we both add words and actions to our common store of sharable realities (as in teaching, criticism, and audiences), and often I surmise from our words that you and I have a real consensus about these public realities. That consensus is what we call "objective" reality (as when we test hallucinations and magicians' tricks), but it did not impose itself on us like an object. Rather, we created it in a dialectic process of re-creating our personal selves from the physical and cultural materials available to us, by means of the four principles by which you have seen H.D., Saul, Sandra, and Seymour compose realities you could share.

Squarely contrary to any theory which begins with the creative and constructive role of human individuality are those which posit for unique, willful humans the same kind of mechanistic cause-effect model that might describe docile minerals and vegetables. The hope, of course, is to isolate a variable here and a variable there and then vary and control them to produce numerical results, predictions, and repeatable experiments. My favorite from the immense bibliography of esthetic studies by such methods is an Italian project in which the experimenters wired up theater seats so that they could measure the frequency with which people wiggled around as they saw different kinds of movies. Fidget frequency. The experimenters then obtained a group of identical twins to watch first a comedy and then a scary movie and then they got some fraternal twins to do the same. The real comedy, I should think, was rows of identical Italian twins all wired up to watch movies and fidget. At any rate, the experimenters concluded that hereditary factors dominated in head posture, while the environment (the shape of the seats perhaps?) seemed to control the position and movement of arm, leg, and rump.[11]

The most familiar of these models using as few variables as possible is, of course, stimulus-response psychology. Organisms passively respond to stimuli, positive and negative reinforcements, operant conditioning, and so on, concepts which Noam Chomsky has elegantly shown are too diffusely defined to describe verbal behavior.[12] Yet, curiously, it is just this limited, unhumanistic stimulus-response approach that some literary critics unconsciously assume. They write as though readers reacted to literary works in one of two ways: appropriately or inappropriately. "Appropriately" means the way the critic reacts, and such literary critics write as though there were certain fixed entities like end-stopped lines or directly presented images or three-part structures (as in "There is a spell") which, because they give rise to a certain effect in the critic, will cause the same effect in everyone—everyone, that is, except those wretches who respond *in*appropriately. *They* need the critic's ministrations.

This kind of right-wrong, on-off model, like the numbers, predictions, and controls which are the tools of the physicalistic psychological experimenter proceed from the assumption that human events are caused in the same way physical events are caused. In particular, they act as though the statement "*A* caused *B*" made the same kind of sense in a context of personalities that it does in a world of physical objects. The experimenter assumes that one can hold everything but *A* constant, vary *A*, and see how *B* varies. Sometimes literary people write as though any sufficiently trained reader should react to a given poem about the same way; that is, holding the poem constant, varying only the training of the reader, the response should vary in accordance with that single variable, training. But in the complex world of literary experience— indeed, in any setting where personality is important—one cannot isolate variables that way.

When we say that *A* is the cause of *B*, we mean that *B* cannot be the cause of *A*—varying *B* will not vary *A*. Yet that is precisely what happened when Sandra and Saul (and Seymour) read "There is a spell." Critics may adopt the convention that literary works cause people's responses, but when you looked at what these three readers actually said, you saw that something much more complicated was going on. To be sure, the poem provided the occasion for the response, but Sandra, Saul, and Seymour poemed their own poem. They re-created H.D.'s creation in terms of their own pattern of drives and defenses according to the principle of multiple function. The response created the poem just as much as the poem created the response. Or you could say it another way: the reader creates the work and then responds to what he has created.

Either way, the psychologist has to give up his ordinary notions of cause and effect, since, here, *A* causes *B and B* causes *A*. He has to give up, therefore, most methods from experimental psychology and, in particular, the simple stimulus-response model that many literary critics tend to assume. Trying to correlate the livelier passages of novels with pulse rate, palmar sweat patterns, even fidget frequency or steroids in the urine, will not do. One is driven to the analysis of personality and response in depth, with all the loss of experimental isolation that entails. Ordinary experiments become pointless because there is no ordinary pattern of causation to test out. We are confronted instead with the complex, overdetermined systems of our own style of reacting with the world.

What we do have—and it is a far richer source of data, I think, than any numbers, even the most multivariate of matrices —is the actual words of the poem and the actual words Sandra and Saul and Seymour used about the poem, together with their introspections and your and my experience of all of this. We were, in effect, in the position of psychoanalysts interpreting a patient's free associations to a dream or symptom. Freud described as early as May 10, 1889, how you do that— the method of free association—and despite all the criticisms heaped on psychoanalysis since, no one has seriously disagreed with that simple method as a window onto mental processes, provided, as in the hearing of a poem, you do not let the substance of the assertions distract you from the choice of words and your own inner response.

The analyst lets his patient talk freely, and he listens for recurring themes in what he hears, mingling his own subjective experience of the patient with what the patient objectively says out loud. Finally, he arrives at an interpretation by understanding those themes as converging toward a single, central issue (which he may or may not say to the patient, depending on the state of the therapy). As Freud wrote in the Wolf-Man case, "The world, [the patient repeatedly] said, was hidden from him by a veil; and our psycho-analytic training forbids our assuming that these words can have been without significance or have been chosen at haphazard." In that same case he insisted, "It is always a strict law of dream-interpretation that an explanation must be found for every detail." In the same way, we have sought central themes and issues in H.D.'s memoir and in the TAT stories, in the interviews with Sandra and Saul, and in Seymour's comments and interpretations of himself. In each instance, we have experienced in miniature what Freud described as the analyst's experience when he has arrived at that central theme or issue for a patient, the feeling of "how, after a certain phase of the treatment, everything seemed to converge upon it, and how later, in the synthesis, the most various and remarkable results radiated out from it; how not only the large problems but the smallest peculiarities in the history of the case were cleared up by this single assumption." [13]

As a recent commentator on psychoanalytic theory puts it, with great exactitude, "Analysis is not concerned with the repeatability of data from case to case, but rather with the inner consistency and pattern of meaning that obtains within each case." "Meaning is the central fact of human existence with which psychoanalysis has to deal. The whole direction of the therapist's effort is toward elaboration of the full context of meaning in which the whole range of data that he has gathered about the patient falls into a consistent, coherent, and intelligible pattern." "This pattern of meaning at its highest level of generalization encompasses the entire life experience of the patient." [14] As it did for H.D. As it began to for Sandra and Saul and Seymour.

Indeed, it is only from this point of view that my work

with Sandra and Saul and the other readers can be called an "experiment." There were many variables I had no way of controlling—for example, what was going on in my readers' lives to affect the way they read these stories and poems, and still more centrally, the way they were adjusting their comments to respond to me. Consciously, I was trying to affect their reading myself as little as possible, but unconsciously I may have been issuing all kinds of cues. We even have an example of my unconscious needs running away with me: my clumsy insistence on an interpretation of the poem which turned Sandra away from it. She expressed her dislike, however, in the same highly individual terms (and in a negative version of the same four principles) with which she had earlier liked the poem.

Further, the important data the interviews provided was not just the gist of Saul's or Sandra's liking or disliking the poem but the exact words they did it in. What cues from me would have encouraged Sandra to see the seathrust as masculine and the tide as feminine? How could a transference toward me have caused Saul to single out the next-to-last five lines or bring in Karl Mundt or shift to a certain poem of escape by Anne Sexton? An interviewer might be able to pressure a reader toward one or another interpretation of the poem or he might be able to cue a liking or disliking, but he cannot alter the fundamental factor in response: the reader's personal style. Because this is the fundamental factor, the aim of an experiment in literary response (indeed, of any psychoanalytic experiment) must be to elicit as much as possible of a subject's personal style, not to slough it off in statistical averages or reduce it by one of the elaborate schemes of content analysis.

In experiments and in general, when we think about humans as personalities, we need to think about the way different processes function toward one central, overall purpose. We need to think, not in terms of isolated causes and effects, but of the convergences of purposes. Apparently, if this picture of reading is correct, and if what applies to reading applies to human experiencing of all kinds, a psychology will not get very far using the physicalistic cause-and-effect thinking appropriate to the hard sciences dealing with physical objects, the kind of thinking that isolates one variable over here and tries to relate it to another isolated variable over there. Rather, Sandra and Saul demand a psychology that recognizes they are total organisms, not "behaviors," and that they are not simply causes and caused but engaged in complex multiple functionings in which a personal style replicates itself over and over until one can see all the details of a life converge like the words in a poem.

That analogy points to a way of looking at people where the literary critic's education and the psychiatrist's should come together. In this matter of making and listening to statements about one's own feelings and personal style and those of others, the psychiatrist and the literary critic can each learn from the other—and should. The literary critic needs to acquire some of the psychiatrist's knowledge about the dynamics of human creation and re-creation. The psychiatrist could profit by learning the literary critic's ways with words: interpretation, analysis, and simply listening. I do not mean using literary characters in lieu of case histories—I do mean listening to what people say, writers included, with that fine attention to detail and nuance in the choice of words which good literary critics pay to what they hear and the repeated synthesis of a great many details into a few centering themes.

The literary critic and the psychiatrist or psychoanalyst differ more in the realms to which they apply their skills than in the skills themselves. Because I am a literary critic, we have been looking at the way people experience literature by re-creating their own inner dynamics through the literary work. But people create their personal style from many different things. Certainly all types of art permit us to transform our unconscious fantasies toward conscious coherence. In the same way, we use vocations and avocations to transform drives into multiply functioning actions on the world. We can adapt unconscious fantasies by means of religious opinions or institutions (like the "Mother" Church). In particular, we use ideas—political, social, philosophical, or ideological beliefs—to transform unconscious fantasies toward conscious, intellectual content. And we use events, to the extent we can "read" them as acting out fantasies the way a novel does (think of the assassination of John F. Kennedy and the needs satisfied by the conspiracy theories projected onto it). We can use even physical objects to transform unconscious content, particularly if we invest them with our personal values, like especially loved cars or dresses or houses. But we use even ordinary objects—as when we dream of them.

Conversely, humans are not the only entities which have a characteristic style of perceiving or acting on reality. Thus Margaret Mead or Ruth Benedict or Erik Erikson could analyze primitive cultures as embodying character traits like the character traits of an individual. Subcultures and organizations within the larger culture, like gangs or corporations, have this quality of transforming many different unconscious aspirations into one central, conscious purpose; the process is analyzed by what is called "functional analysis," which is very like the thematic analysis of a personality. Similarly, entire nations transform fantasies into immense actions and styles, as in many recent studies of what is now called "political culture" (to avoid the impressionism associated with the older but more accurate term, "national character").[15]

We began by trying to systematize the way people create and re-create purely literary experiences, but we found a principle with scope enough to apply to any situation where a personality, single or collective, experiences some other reality, a culture, a work of art, an organization, a nation, another person, or simply a thing. This is what the psychoanalysis of literature implies: once we cease making literature an isolated, formalistic set of variables, once we insist that it is an organic experience in the minds of men and a part of the great continuum of human experiences, then rigorous thinking about literature leads us into very large questions indeed. Our traditional methods of response, the quest for individual unities and continuing styles, become, as they should, ways to understand the most central processes of human life.

A being with a character experiences reality only to the extent he can give it life within that character. Poems and theories, groups and cultures, fictions and criticism, teaching and films, people in general, works of art—we experience them all, we and everything that has a personal style, by creating that style from the words and things they offer us. The "psychoanalysis of literature" all by itself is a contradiction in terms. One cannot study literature as such psychoanalytically, only "poems in persons," literature in some human being, the one who made it, the one who is experiencing it, the one who is talking about it. This book, too—I have created it, but before it can take on validity for you, you have to re-create it in your individual style. That will depend on the extent to which you can find your patterns of adaptation and gratification in my words, the limits they outline, and the freedoms they invite. Thus this book ends where it began. People are the natural habitat of literature—and finally of literary theories as well.

A Polemical Epilogue and
Brief Guide to Further Reading

SINCE THE FIRST psychoanalytic study of literature took place three quarters of a century ago (about October 15, 1897), it is with some sense of irony that I call this book an "introduction." The psychoanalysis of literature has progressed in that time, along with psychoanalysis itself, far more than its potential audience seems to know. In the early decades of this century even well informed people met psychoanalysis with simplicity, suspicion, and downright savagery. The savagery has fallen off, but misunderstandings are almost as common today (although, to be sure, their style has changed). It is my and my fellow adventurers' further misfortune that, within psychoanalysis, there is no application so widely misconceived and misdescribed, so subjected to the prejudices of litterateurs and psychologists as the psychoanalysis of literature. An introduction, alas, is still in order, some demystification, some opening up to the theoretical breakthroughs of the last twenty-five years or so, which seem largely to have gone unnoticed outside psychoanalytic circles themselves.

Psychoanalysis as a therapy, of course, looks much as it always has, and it suffers today many of the same handicaps and difficulties as in Freud's time. Pure psychoanalysis (as a therapy) may well be replaced by the partially adequate substitutes it has fathered, and psychoanalysis as such may continue to exist only as a way of training specialists. Psychoanalytic theory, however, particularly in the last twenty-five years, has advanced to become the only psychology capable of a comprehensive view of man that spans the largest social and philosophical issues and the most precise clinical questions, especially people's choices of particular words.

Perhaps because this intellectual achievement is coming to be dimly apprehended, psychoanalysis in the sixties and seventies has gained an all-too-eager acceptance in some circles. But what gets accepted is a curiously hybrid "Freudianism," compounded of the earliest strata of psychoanalytic theory and the "latest" from the Seventh Avenue of intellectual fashion. That is, one finds the oedipus complex but little else in infantile development (although Freud discovered the other pre-oedipal stages in 1913 and 1915). One finds phallic, vaginal, or anal symbols (and no other kinds) in an abundance that could be achieved only by someone who had read little more than Chapter X of the *Introductory Lectures* (1915–1917) or Chapter IV-E of *The Interpretation of Dreams* (mostly added in 1909 and 1911).

Tacked onto this *ur-Freudismus* are scraps of later theory. The death instinct exerts its usual mesmeric influence. A superego may be introduced but treated as though it were merely a social, political, cultural, or intellectual influence. The latest theory of schizophrenia will jostle an "ego psychology" that simply writes off the id so painfully visible in that very schizophrenia. Then there are the gurus. "Existentialists," "third force psychologists," "encounter leaders," Reich, Marcuse, Laing, Lacan, Perls, and so on—people treat them as quick, bright alternatives to a black magic fantasied about "Freud" or "orthodox psychoanalysis."

Nothing, however, could be more alien to the honest self-examination psychoanalysis demands than the hope of miraculous gimmicks or the substitution of word magic for hard realities. Psychoanalysis is neither white magic nor black, neither abstract discourse nor some unspeakable mystery on the bestial couch. The popular success of the gimmicks and the gurus testify all too sadly to that deep, driving hunger in every man for something that will lift him—us—above the limitations all humans share. I am reminded of Freud's wise caution that, before writing or passing judgment on psychoanalytic matters, one should have some actual experience of psychoanalytic insight—most of all, I should think, of that terrible, narcissistic hunger for omnipotence. For a long time, of course, this was not possible. Now that some analytic institutes have opened their doors to nonmedical people, alas, the very intellectuals who could profit most from this education seem less willing than ever to admit they do not know everything about anything at all.

When applied to literature, a cookbook psychoanalysis leads to a heavy reliance on symbolism, usually just phallic or anal symbols (with no heed paid to the cautions about symbolic interpretation Freud kept adding to successive editions of *The Interpretation of Dreams*). The critic points to oedipal patterns but few others, and finally he simply awards his approval to those works or characters that live up to the ethical values he or his guru favor. The rest he dismisses as hopelessly mired in repression, hypocrisy, imperialism, or rationality. Some analysts have themselves added shoddy literary work, totally unprovable statements about authors' lives, or diagnoses of characters, their motives, dreams, and neuroses, as though they had walked out of the pages of fiction into a psychiatric clinic. Conversely—and surprisingly—analysts will often settle (as few literary people would) for a kind of Sunday-morning reverence about Art-with-a-capital-*A* that seems simply to provide a new future for an old illusion.

What all this leaves out is the brilliant synthesis psychoanalysis has made, beginning with Freud's earliest case histories but not culminating until the 1960s. As the teachings of psychoanalysis became better known in the thirties and forties, the old isolated hysterical and obsessional symptoms ceased to be ego-acceptable solutions to conflicts. Patients felt their sufferings rather as a series of recurring problems that pervaded a whole life, character disorders instead of discrete "neuroses." Therapy, therefore, evolved into "character analysis." Theory, drawing on this change in the therapeutic experience, began to conceptualize, not isolated symptoms, but the whole human being. Child observation and treatment showed people developing through oral, anal, phallic, and oedipal stages, with each stage building on the achievements—and failures—of its predecessors. It became possible to understand a person as a continuing "ego identity" or "identity theme" like a musical theme and variations. The ego, once thought of as the helpless rider on a willful horse, came to be understood as a forceful mediator among the other psychic agencies and the world beyond. All its moves had a "multiple function," and therefore whatever an individual thought or did came to be seen as a compromise between the demands of inner and outer reality.

Today patients (in the affluent society anyway) present a further shift. They see themselves suffering not so much from disorders of character as problems in their relations with others. Accordingly, theory now is extending the synthesis of the sixties, the *intra*psychic concepts of "identity" and "multiple function," into the *inter*psychic world of human relations, culture, society, government, and history. But the theory has already been built, and it seems unlikely to me that the seventies, despite a more social emphasis, will produce any great theoretical departures from the comprehensive view of man achieved by psychoanalysis in the sixties.

When this large synthesis comes to literature, four important insights follow, four radical improvements over the older approach through a psychoanalysis directed primarily to symptoms and symbols. First, one recognizes that the unconscious content we project into literature does not consist simply of a bevy of phalluses or vaginas and the dire doings of oedipal mothers and fathers. It includes not isolated symbols but coherent fantasies and these from pre-oedipal stages as well as oedipal. What may appear fragmentary in oedipal terms will necessarily serve as a coherent fantasy at some pre-oedipal level. There will be a coherence and convergence of fantasy, if one takes into account all the levels of one's infantile unconscious participating in the literary transaction.

Second, reading or writing literature is an act of *transformation*. Just as the ego in a man's daily life transforms drives, so, in reading or writing, it transforms the unconscious fantasies he projects into the text. Just as, in human development, each stage provides the groundwork for the next, so, in the literary transaction, one's fantasies at "higher" levels represent transformations of more primitive fantasies associated with the earliest levels of human development. In particular, just as, in human development, the first stage with its crucial issues of ambivalence, basic trust, and self-object differentiation provides the foundation for all subsequent stages, so, in creating and re-creating literature, one makes at least some themes and issues from that first stage pervade every literary work. This is the reason it has been possible to build this entire book upon variations of a single oral fantasy.

Third, once one acknowledges that creating and re-creating literature transforms unconscious fantasies, then it becomes possible to talk psychologically about what used to be thought purely literary entities, because they are what we use to achieve this transformation. As we have seen, just as the transformation in reading and writing resembles the human's transformation of his drives, so literary *themes* are what he derives from his constant press of unconscious material toward conscious expression and intellectual synthesis. So literary *forms* are the various defense mechanisms and adaptive strategies his ego has synthesized from the materials of the text. Without any concept of form, the psychoanalysis of literature had to confine itself pretty closely to narratives with oedipal content. With a sense of both theme and form, psychoanalysis can deal even with nonfiction prose or, as we have seen, lyric poems.

Fourth, and somewhat paradoxically, having seen how people create and re-create literary works out of their wholly personal style and identity, one can go on to understand the connection between literature and its political, economic, intellectual, and other nonpersonal "backgrounds" to which most theorists give such importance. Both writer and reader use these backgrounds as the great reservoir of raw material with which they continually synthesize their identity themes and add new experiences (for example, of writing or reading) to their pre-existing lifestyles. Yet those lifestyles were themselves built up from a series of such syntheses dating back to the mother-child relationship. Once one can speak at all of an ego style (after self-object differentiation, that is), then at any given moment the ego is determining how cultural and other backgrounds will enter into that ego. It is this personality, then, built up from the quite personal absorption of "backgrounds" by the principles of synthesis we have seen, that creates and re-creates literature.

The idea of character as an identity theme and variations on it presupposes a continuous, mutual development of personality and political, social, economic, cultural, and other impersonal backgrounds. To ask which determines the other is like asking whether the chicken or the egg came first—it depends on how you look at it. From the larger point of view I am suggesting, that question ceases to matter. It is in this sense that one can, as so many have tried to do, "create a synthesis of Marx and Freud"—although it would be more accurate to speak of combining cultural and psychological determinisms.

Finally, then, what this new psychoanalytic look at literature comes to is a series of rich analogies and connections
between literature and life. One can no longer think psychoanalytically in terms of a congeries of phalluses, orifices, castra-
tions, rapes, murders, myths, and madnesses, but of a continuum that reaches from the *bizarrerie* of the depths to the
highest or most realistic—and even the commonplace—thoughts
of consciousness. A nightmare seethes inside the everyday, but
to take either without the other is to make both false. One must
find the continuing center of one's being in literature as well as
life. In this quest, psychoanalysis serves not as a codebook or a
philosophical system but as a way of becoming aware of one's
own reactions to people, experiences, and books.

How much one can learn this kind of psychoanalysis just
from reading, I do not know. Freud was unquestionably right
to insist that a full understanding of psychoanalysis requires
that one experience it, but, of course, only a few can do that.
A "reading knowledge" of psychoanalysis creates little more
than an illusion of understanding. Something more, I think,
but anyone suggesting readings (as I am about to) does so
knowing he is substituting books for people. I shall try, anyway, to stress as much as I can the human reality of psychoanalysis rather than metapsychological schemata or "Freudian"
codebooks.

On this principle, next to analysis itself, the best introduction to psychoanalysis comes from a reading of Freud's case
histories. Unmatched in their extraordinary observations, they
should be read rather for insights into the individual patients
than for their theoretical generalizations (many of which have
been improved on since). And, of course, if they cannot be
read in German, they should be read in the splendid Strachey
translation or in one of the reprints derived from it: *The
Standard Edition of the Complete Psychological Works of
Sigmund Freud,* trans. and ed. James Strachey, Anna Freud,

Alix Strachey, and Alan Tyson, 24 vols. (London: The Hogarth Press, 1953—).* Some of the earlier English translations actually falsify Freud's statements, and not even the German *Gesammelte Werke* has the scholarly aids of the English edition.

Of the five major case histories, I find "Rat Man" the most assimilable. The *Standard Edition* includes a sizable segment of Freud's original record of the case, fascinating as much for what he could not see (because he had not yet discovered the importance, for example, of orality) as for what he did see and so brilliantly interpret: "Notes upon a Case of Obsessional Neurosis" (1909), *Std. Ed.*, X, 153–318.

"Wolf-Man" is another obsessional. Freud originally analyzed him from 1910 to 1914: "From the History of an Infantile Neurosis" (1918 [1914]), *Std. Ed.*, XVII, 3–122. "Wolf-Man," however, holds the unique honor of being the longest longitudinal study in psychiatric annals. A recent collection brings together materials on him from the age of six months to eighty-five years: *The Wolf-Man by the Wolf-Man* (New York: Basic Books, 1971). The collection includes the *Standard Edition* translation of the case and provides the most striking illustration I know of the continuity of a personal myth or identity theme.

The other major cases, Little Hans, Dora, and Schreber, all have their special features: "Analysis of a Phobia in a Five-Year-Old-Boy" (1909), *Std. Ed.*, X, 3–149; "Fragment of an Analysis of a Case of Hysteria" (1905 [1901]), *Std. Ed.*, VII, 3–122; "Psycho-Analytic Notes on an Autobiographical

---

* W. W. Norton publishes (based on the Strachey edition) Freud's *An Autobiographical Study, Civilization and Its Discontents, The Complete Introductory Lectures on Psychoanalysis, The Ego and the Id, Jokes and Their Relation to the Unconscious, Leonardo da Vinci and a Memory of His Childhood, New Introductory Lectures on Psycho-Analysis, On Dreams, On the History of the Psycho-Analytic Movement, An Outline of Psychoanalysis, The Problem of Anxiety, The Psychopathology of Everyday Life,* and *Totem and Taboo.*

Account of a Case of Paranoia" (1911), *Std. Ed.*, XIII, 3–82.
Dora, in particular, has been restudied by Erikson from the
point of view of contemporary thinking about adolescence:
Erik Erikson, "Psychological Reality and Historical Actuality"
in *Insight and Responsibility* (New York: W. W. Norton and
Co., 1964). All three cases, however, will yield the kind of
centering "myth" we have seen for H.D.

Once we go beyond the five classic case histories, matters
become very large and very confusing very fast. I am tempted
to say, "Well, you should read all of Freud, Anna Freud, Jones,
Abraham, Fenichel, Ferenczi, Erikson—and then there are
these classic papers by other people. . . ." But this is of little
help to someone seeking a realistic introduction, not total im-
mersion in a year's reading.

The classic introduction is, of course, Freud's own *Introductory Lectures*, but brilliant and challenging as they are, I
am inclined to think they have begun to do more harm than
good when read by students and laymen as their only contact
with today's psychoanalysis. One would find nothing about
the eat-and-be-eaten fantasy of merger which has played such
an important part in this book, for example, but one would
find considerable emphasis on the mouth as a symbol for the
vagina. What so many laymen have carried away from the
Introductory Lectures is a codebook of symbolism, with which
they make a travesty of psychoanalysis by crude one-to-one
interpretations that quite lose the individual subjectivity which
is, after all, what psychoanalysis is about.

Consider, for example, the image of the seashell with
which we have had so much to do. Were I to consult the
"Index of Symbols" in the *Standard Edition* of Freud's *Introductory Lectures*, I would be led to a list including pits, cavi-
ties, hollows, vessels, bottles, receptacles, boxes, trunks, cases,
chests, pockets, ships, cupboards, stoves, and rooms—and
finally, the sentence, "Among animals, *snails* and *mussels* at

least are undeniably female symbols," and not far after, "*Jewel* and *treasure* are used in dreams as well as in waking life to describe someone who is loved." If I were simply to establish similar one-to-one equations for "seashell" or "pearl-of-great-price," I do not know how I would deal with the complex, over-determined experiences that went into the writing of the poem (where H.D. seems to associate the seashell with a body imprisoning but protecting a creative soul) or the readings, where Sandra found the shell something to be filled with reality and not cut off from it and Seymour sought an escape into its hardness and geometry. All these nuances—all the life in the creation and re-creation of the poem—would be lost by a mere dreambook decoding. Nevertheless, many people today still need Freud's cautions on symbolism in *The Interpretation of Dreams:*

I should like to utter an express warning against over-estimating the importance of symbols in dream-interpretation, against restricting the work of translating dreams merely to translating symbols and against abandoning the technique of making use of the dreamer's associations. The two techniques of dream-interpretation must be complementary to each other; but both in practice and in theory the first place continues to be held by the procedure . . . which attributes a decisive significance to the comments made by the dreamer.

The first requirement of any introduction to psychoanalysis for laymen should be Freud's continuing awareness of the human realities that underlie psychoanalytic insight.

What I would also like to see in a general introduction to psychoanalysis is a full account of the phases of childhood development (oral, anal, phallic, oedipal); the structural theory (id, ego, superego); the signal theory of anxiety that gave rise to it; an expanded concept of defense (not just repression but projection, reaction-formation, and the others we would need to comment on a variety of literary works); most important, the modern psychoanalytic concept of character we used to approach H.D. and our two readers. In addition, I would like the reader to get some feeling for the cases a psychoanalyst deals with, some sense of the experience of psychoanalysis, and a little knowledge of psychoanalysis as an institution (its training institutes, the American Psychoanalytic Association, the International Psycho-Analytical Association, and so on). Any one of the following books will serve. I have listed them in order of preference:

Ives Hendrick, *Facts and Theories of Psychoanalysis*, 3rd. ed., rev. (New York: Knopf, 1958)

Robert Waelder, *Basic Theory of Psychoanalysis* (New York: International Universities Press, 1960)

Franz Alexander, *Fundamentals of Psychoanalysis* (New York: Norton, 1948)

Morton Levitt, ed., *Readings in Psychoanalytic Psychology* (New York: Appleton-Century-Crofts, 1959)

Charles Brenner, *An Elementary Textbook of Psychoanalysis* (Garden City: Doubleday-Anchor, 1957)

None of these has the boldness and vigor of Freud's own introduction, but they all contain much he did not know in 1917. I think the time has come to admit that Freud's *Introductory Lectures* must be taken as an index to his thinking at a certain point in time (thinking he himself revised) and that it can no longer serve as an introduction to psychoanalysis now.

Because of the singular importance of the concept of character or personality or "ego identity" or "identity theme" in today's psychoanalysis, both clinical and applied, I list here some important articles (and hope that the modern library can make them available). The first we have referred to repeatedly in the course of this book: Robert Waelder, "The Principle of Multiple Function: Observations on Over-Determination," *Psychoanalytic Quarterly*, V (1936), 45–62. The most eloquent and far-reaching of the papers to derive from Waelder's fundamental statement of the adaptive hypothesis are by Erik Erikson, and I particularly recommend those collected in Erik H. Erikson, *Identity and the Life Cycle, Psychological Issues*, I (1959), 1–171. The most rigorous theoretical development of the concept of identity occurs in Heinz Lichtenstein, "Identity and Sexuality: A Study of Their Interrelationship in Man," *Journal of the American Psychoanalytic Association*, IX (1961), 179–260. A recent article showing the kinds of radical simplifications that result from Waelder's principle is Roy Schafer, "The Mechanisms of Defence," *International Journal of Psycho-Analysis*, XLIX (1968), 49–62. As it turns out, because the mechanisms of defense correspond (roughly) to forms in the arts, his essay shows why, as critics have long said, form and content are inseparable.

When we turn from clinical psychoanalysis to the psychoanalysis of literature, we find the same great bulk of material. I could easily recommend a hundred essays, some, obviously, of more use or relevance than others. Since this is a quidditative guide to further study, I shall try to pare readings to some essential minimum. Even so, I would be less than candid if I did not urge on you the two larger books from which this small one comes: Norman N. Holland, *The Dynamics of Literary Response* (New York: Oxford University Press, 1968) and Norman N. Holland, *5 Readers Reading* (in preparation). My own applications of psychoanalysis to literature partly build upon two still earlier books, the first very rigorously theoretical, the second more humanistic and flexible: Ernst Kris, *Psychoanalytic Explorations in Art* (New York: International Universities Press, 1952); Simon O. Lesser, *Fiction and the Unconscious* (Boston: Beacon Press, 1957). As with clinical psychoanalysis, one could extend this list for yards, but I am trying to offer the absolute minimum that would make an entering wedge into the field.

Psychoanalytic criticism is like Longfellow's little girl: when she was good, she was very, very good, but when she was bad, she was horrid. Perhaps the best way to sample psychoanalytic criticism, good, bad, and horrid, is to browse through one or another of the anthologies. I say "browse," and only on that basis do I list four:

Frederick C. Crews, ed., *Psychoanalysis & Literary Process* (Cambridge, Mass.: Winthrop Publishers, 1970)
Leonard and Eleanor Manheim, eds., *Hidden Patterns* (New York: The Macmillan Company, 1966)
William Phillips, ed., *Art and Psychoanalysis* (New York: Criterion Books, 1957)
Hendrik M. Ruitenbeek, ed., *Psychoanalysis and Literature* (New York: E. P. Dutton, 1964)

In browsing, I would suggest some criteria for telling lilies from weeds. First, does the author recognize that we perceive both conscious, intellectual content as well as unconscious fantasies in literary works and deal with both? Or does he settle for the "secret, unconscious meaning" rigmarole? Does he treat the formal aspects? Does he have a sense of the "style" or essence or "character" of the work? Does he deal with what the text says or translate it immediately and reductively by means of a symbolic decoding? All these questions combine, really, in one. Does he deal with the *language?* For the great thing psychoanalysis brings to the study of literature—something no other psychology offers—is a way to understand a writer's— and a reader's—choice of words.

Most people applying psychoanalysis to literature do so to study one particular writer or work rather than to develop a theory. Again, a list of such studies would be very long; the simplest thing is a bibliographical algorithm. Two basic bibliographies are Norman Kiell, *Psychoanalysis, Psychology, and Literature* (Madison: University of Wisconsin Press, 1963)

✓ procedure, system

and Alexander Grinstein, *Index of Psychoanalytic Writings,* 12 vols. (New York: International Universities Press, 1956—   ). Running bibliographies appear in: *Literature and Psychology, Psychological Abstracts,* the *Journal of Aesthetics and Art Criticism, Psychoanalytic Quarterly,* and the standard literary bibliographies (e.g., *PMLA* or *Abstracts of English Studies*). I would repeat my criterion. To what extent does a given article deal with the particular words of the work it studies?

The above is, I realize, a very brief guide indeed. It "requires" perhaps two of Freud's case histories, one general introduction to psychoanalysis, four articles on the concept of character, two books on the applications of psychoanalysis to literature, and a browse through some psycho-literary anthologies. In being so short, I am trying to offer a realistic start in the field rather than a display of eclecticism or erudition, a list someone could actually read who was just beginning to be interested.

Once he goes beyond some such beginning core as this, the next "requirements" might well include as many as fifty books and articles. Such a list, moreover, begins to go out of date within a few months of drawing it up, and I have not, therefore, tried to present one here. To obtain a longer reading list which will be current and which will have some guidelines as to sequence, the reader should write to The Center for the Psychological Study of the Arts, Faculty of Arts and Letters, State University of New York at Buffalo, Buffalo, N.Y., 14214. There—here—such lists are prepared and kept up to date for successive semesters of students and faculty and their continuing researches. Contributions are welcome.

Notes

ONE — A MAKER'S MIND

I HAVE PROFITED greatly from the discussions of this paper that took place at the Buffalo Group for Applied Psychoanalysis and the Seminar in Critical Theory, July, 1971, at the State University of New York at Buffalo. In the same way, three earlier versions of this material have encouraged me to put my thoughts on H.D. together, each time with a somewhat different emphasis: "Freud and H.D.," *International Journal of Psycho-Analysis*, L (1969), 309–315; "H.D. et Freud," *Études freudiennes*, Nos. 3–4, Septembre 1970, pp. 143–156; and especially "H.D. and the 'Blameless Physician,'" *Contemporary Literature*, Volume 10, Number 4 (© 1969 by the Regents of the University of Wisconsin), pp. 474–506. I am grateful to the University of Wisconsin Press for permission to reprint parts of that version in this chapter.

1. Unless otherwise indicated, all poems are taken from *Collected Poems of H.D.*, 2nd ed. (New York: Boni and Liveright, 1940).

2. Joseph N. Riddel, "H.D. and the Poetics of 'Spiritual Realism,'" *Contemporary Literature*, X (Autumn, 1969), 447–473. This entire issue of *CL* is devoted to H.D. and contains useful bibliographies as well as memoirs, letters, and articles. I am much indebted to Professor Riddel for letting me consult

his essay during the writing of mine.

3. *Tribute to Freud* (New York: Pantheon Books, 1956). I shall quote a great deal from this book. Those wishing to trace the quotations to their source should consult an earlier, more fully documented version of this essay mentioned above, "H.D. and the 'Blameless Physician,'" *Contemporary Literature*, X (Autumn, 1969), 474–506, or, better yet, the memoir itself.

4. W. B. Yeats, "At Stratford-on-Avon," *Ideas of Good and Evil* (London: A. H. Bullen, 1903), pp. 161–162.

5. Horace Gregory, Introduction to *Helen in Egypt by H.D.* (New York: Grove Press, 1961), p. ix. H.D., *The Walls Do Not Fall* (London: Oxford University Press, 1944), p. 40.

6. *Helen in Egypt*, p. 188.

7. H.D., *Palimpsest* (Paris: Contact Editions, 1926), p. 218.

8. *Helen in Egypt*, pp. 23, 271, et al.

9. Thomas B. Swann, *The Classical World of H.D.* (Lincoln, Neb.: University of Nebraska Press, 1962), pp. 62 and 36. I am drawing extensively on Professor Swann's book. I have also consulted Vincent Quinn, *Hilda Doolittle (H.D.)*, Twayne's United States Authors Series (New York: Twayne Publishers, Inc. 1967).

10. Riddel, *op cit.*, pp. 469–470 and 447–448.

11. *The Autobiography of William Carlos Williams* (New York: New Directions Books, 1951), p. 67.

12. Swann, *op. cit.*, p. 19.

13. Williams, *op. cit.*, pp. 190 and 219.

14. Swann, *op. cit.*, p. 20.

15. Bryher [Winifred Ellerman], *The Heart to Artemis: A Writer's Memoirs* (New York: Harcourt, Brace, and World, 1962), pp. 263–264.

16. On the length of analysis: Freud, "Analysis Terminable and Interminable" (1937), *Std. Ed.*, XXIII, 209–253. Ernest Jones, *International Journal of Psycho-Analysis*, XXXVII (1957), 126. Freud's remark about Mahler

occurs in a letter of January 4, 1935, reprinted in Theodor Reik, *The Haunting Melody: Psychoanalytic Experiences in Life and Music* (New York: 1953).

17. *Helen in Egypt*, pp. 23, 260, 271.

18. Freud, *Std. Ed.*, XXIII, 252.

19. Erik Erikson, *Young Man Luther* (New York: W. W. Norton, 1958), pp. 263–266; the quotation in the text is from p. 264.

20. "Toward the Piraeus," *Collected Poems*, pp. 263–264.

21. Among the many psychoanalysts and analytical psychologists who have come to this conclusion are: Freud, "Medusa's Head" (1940 [1922]),*Std. Ed.*, XVIII, 273–274, and "The Infantile Genital Organization" (1923), *Std. Ed.*, XIX, 144; Sandor Ferenczi, "On the Symbolism of the Head of Medusa" (1923) in *Further Contributions to the Theory and Technique of Psycho-Analysis* (London: Hogarth Press, 1926), p. 360; Otto Fenichel, "The Scoptophilic Instinct and Identification"(1935), *The Collected Papers of Otto Fenichel, First Series* (New York: W. W. Norton, 1953), pp. 389–391; Erich Neumann, *The Great Mother: An Analysis of the Archetype* (New York: Pantheon Books, 1955), pp. 166–170 and Plates 70, 80, 100; Erik Erikson, "The Nature of Clinical Evidence" in *Insight and Responsibility* (New York: W. W. Norton, 1964), p. 70.

22. H.D., *By Avon River* (New York: Macmillan, 1949), p. 35.

23. "Hermes of the Ways," *Collected Poems*, p. 57.

24. London: Brendin Publishing Co., 1936.

25. *Tribute to the Angels* (New York: Oxford University Press, 1945), p. 17.

26. *Ibid.*, p. 19.

27. Sandor Ferenczi, "The Ontogenesis of the Interest in Money" in *Contributions to Psychoanalysis* (Boston: Richard C. Badger, 1916), Freud, *The Interpretation of Dreams* (1900–1901), *Std. Ed.*, V, 403.

28. *Tribute to the Angels*, pp. 33–34.

29. *The Walls Do Not Fall*, p. 12.

30. *Ibid.*, p. 18.

31. *Ibid.*, p. 23.

32. Robert Waelder, "The Principle of Multiple Function," *Psychoanalytic Quarterly*, V (1936), 45–62. Summarized in Otto Fenichel, *The Psychoanalytic Theory of Neurosis* (New York: W. W. Norton, 1945), p. 467.

33. " 'Civilized' Sexual Morality and Modern Nervous Illness" (1908), *Std. Ed.*, IX, 198.

34. Abram Kardiner and Associates, *The Psychological Frontiers of Society* (New York: Columbia University Press, 1945), p. 372.

35. Heinz Hartmann, *Psychoanalysis and Moral Values*, The Freud Anniversary Lecture Series, The New York Psychoanalytic Institute (New York: International Universities Press, 1960). On prose style, see the series of papers on language by Maria Lorenz and Stanley Cobb in *A.M.A. Archives of Neurology and Psychiatry*, LXIX–LXX (1952–53); or Norman N. Holland, "Prose and Minds: A Psychoanalytic Approach to Non-Fiction" in *The Art of Victorian Prose*, ed. George Levine and William Madden (New York: Oxford University Press, 1968), pp. 314–337; also the works of Richard Ohmann noted in this last essay. For cognitive styles, see Anna Freud, "Obsessional Neurosis: A Summary of Psycho-Analytic Views as Presented at the Congress," *International Journal of Psycho-Analysis*, XLVII (1966), 116–122, 120.

36. Roy Schafer, "The Mechanisms of Defence," *International Journal of Psycho-Analysis*, XLIX (1968), 49–62.

37. Roy Schafer, "An Overview of Heinz Hartmann's Contributions to Psychoanalysis," *International Journal of Psycho-Analysis*, LI (1970), 425–446, especially 438–442. On the question of style as a variable, see Norman N. Holland, "The Art of Scientific Biography," *Kenyon Review*, XXX (1968), 702–707.

38. Fenichel, *The Psychoanalytic Theory of Neurosis*, p. 467.

39. Herbert Fingarette, *The Self in Transformation: Psychoanalysis, Philosophy, and the Life of the Spirit* (New York: Basic Books, 1963), pp. 20–21.

40. Freud, "From the History of an Infantile Neurosis" (1918 [1914]), *Std. Ed.*, XVII, 52.

41. Heinz Lichtenstein, "Identity and Sexuality: A Study of Their Interrelationship in Man," *Journal of the American Psychoanalytic Association*, IX (1961), 179–260. Alexander Thomas, Stella Chess, and Herbert G. Birch, "The Origin of Personality," *Scientific American*, CCIII

(August, 1970), 102–109. David Shapiro, *Neurotic Styles*, Austen Riggs Center Monographs No. 5 (New York: Basic Books, 1965), p. 179.

42. Heinz Lichtenstein, "The Role of Narcissism in the Emergence and Maintenance of a Primary Identity," *International Journal of Psycho-Analysis*, XLV (1964), 49–56; "Towards a Metapsychological Definition of the Concept of Self," *ibid.*, XLVI (1965), 117–128.

43. Lichtenstein, "Identity and Sexuality."

44. Erik Erikson, *Identity and the Life Cycle, Psychological Issues*, I (1959), No. 1, Monograph 1, p. 26. See also Lichtenstein, "The Dilemma of Human Identity: Notes on Self-Transformation, Self-Objectivation, and Metamorphosis," *Journal of the American Psychoanalytic Association*, XI (1963), 173–223.

45. Lichtenstein, "Towards a Metapsychological Definition of the Concept of Self," p. 119.

46. Letter from H.D., quoted by Norman Holmes Pearson in her posthumous volume of poetry, *Hermetic Definition* (New York: New Directions Books, 1972), p. vi. See also Norman Holmes Pearson, "An Interview on H.D.," *Contemporary Literature*, X (Autumn, 1969), 445. I have repunctuated the quotation to remove an ambiguity.

47. Swann, *op. cit.*, p. 10.

48. *Contemporary Literature*, X (Autumn, 1969), 605–626.

49. Norman N. Holland, *The Dynamics of Literary Response* (New York: Oxford University Press, 1968), pp. 239–241.

50. See, for example, John Rickman, "On the Nature of Ugliness and the Creative Impulse," *International Journal of Psycho-Analysis*, XXI (1940), 294–313.

51. "From the History of an Infantile Neurosis" (1918 [1914]), *Std. Ed.*, XVII, 105–106.

Two — TWO READERS' MINDS

As WITH THE preceding chapter, I am grateful for having been able to present and discuss these ideas with a variety of audiences; with the Michigan Association for Psychoanalysis, a very early version; at the Mental Health Research Center of New York University; before the students and faculty of the Departments of English, Trinity College, the Université de Bordeaux III, and the Institut d'Anglais of the Université de Paris VII. Readers of *5 Readers Reading* will recognize in this chapter a segment of that long experimental study supported by grants from the Research Foundation, State University of New York, and the Commission on Obscenity and Pornography. In arriving at the approach to subjectivity embodied in this chapter and the next, I have been profoundly influenced by the ideas of David Bleich.

1. This experiment is described in much greater detail in Chapter III of my *5 Readers Reading* (in preparation).

2. Sandra herself is described in more detail in Chapter IV of *5 Readers Reading*, and her responses to three other literary works are analyzed in Chapters VI, VII, and VIII.

3. H.D., *The Walls Do Not Fall* (London: Oxford University Press, 1944), p. 12. The book is a lyric cycle of linked poems —hence the "for instance" in the first line.

4. "Literature's Gratifying Dead End," *Hudson Review,* XXI (1968), 774–775.

5. Roy Schafer, *Aspects of Internalization* (New York: International Universities Press, 1968), pp. 91–104.

6. Like Sandra, Saul's personality is analyzed in more detail in Chapter IV of *5 Readers Reading*; Chapters VI and VIII deal with his responses to two other literary works.

7. Norman N. Holland, *The Dynamics of Literary Response* (New York: Oxford University Press, 1968).

THREE — MY MIND AND YOURS

I AM GRATEFUL FOR several occasions on which I could give an early version of this chapter in lecture form with an opportunity for questions and discussion. Some of these took place with psychiatric audiences: at the Psychiatric Services of the New England Medical Hospital and the Beth Israel Hospital, both in Boston. Other occasions were literary: at Gannon College, Northern Illinois University, the University of Pittsburgh, Temple University, and the University of Massachusetts at Amherst. Finally, this chapter has been much changed from a shorter and conceptually different version, "The 'Unconscious' of Literature: The Psychoanalytic Approach," in *Contemporary Criticism*, ed. Malcolm Bradbury and David Palmer,

Stratford-Upon-Avon Studies 12 (London: Edward Arnold, 1970), pp. 131–153.

1. From *Lunch Poems*, The Pocket Poets Series: Number 19 (San Francisco: City Lights Books, 1964), p. 27.
2. "The Moses of Michelangelo" (1914), *Std. Ed.*, XIII, 211. See also Ernest Jones, *The Life and Work of Sigmund Freud*, 3 vols. (New York: Basic Books, 1953–57), II, 367. Northrop Frye, "Literary Criticism," in *The Aims and Methods of Scholarship in Modern Languages and Literatures*, ed. James Thorpe (New York: Modern Language Association of America, 1963), p. 57.
3. Paul Carroll, *The Poem in Its Skin* (Chicago and New York: Follett Publishing Co., 1968), pp. 160–163.
4. Solomon E. Asch, "Opinions and Social Pressure," in *Frontiers of Psychological Research*, ed. Stanley Coopersmith (San Francisco: W. H. Freeman and Co., 1966), pp. 107–111. The article is reporting on a continuing line of investigation by others as well as Asch.
5. Robert Waelder, "The Principle of Multiple Function: Observations on Over-Determination," *Psychoanalytic Quarterly*, V (1936), 45–62, 56. For a more clinical discussion, see Karl Abraham, "The Influence of Oral Erotism on Character Formation" (1924) in *On Character and Libido Development, Six Essays*, ed. Bertram D. Lewin (New York: W. W. Norton, 1966), pp. 151–164.
6. See Abraham, *op. cit.*
7. "Creative Writers and Day-

Dreaming" (1908), *Std. Ed.*, IX, 143–153, 153.
8. D. W. Winnicott, "Transitional Objects and Transitionl Phenomena," in *Playing and Reality* (London: Tavistock Publications, 1971), pp. 1–25. By the same author, "The Location of Cultural Experience," *International Journal of Psycho-Analysis*, XLVIII (1966), 368–372.
9. Herman A. Witkin, "The Perception of the Upright," in *Frontiers of Psychological Research*. ed. Stanley Coopersmith (San Francisco: W. H. Freeman and Co., 1966), pp. 186–192. T. G. R. Bower, "The Visual World of Infants," *Scientific American*, CCXV (December, 1966), 80–92. David Noton and Lawrence Stark, "Eye Movements and Visual Perception," *Scientific American*, CCXXIV (June, 1971), 35–43. Paul A. Kolers, "Experiments in Reading," *Scientific American*, CCXXVII (July, 1972), 84–91.
10. Jerome Kagan, "Do Infants Think?" *Scientific American*, CCXXVI (March, 1972), 74–82. Jean Piaget, *The Origins of Intelligence in Children*, trans. Margaret Cook (New York: W. W. Norton and Co., 1963). George A. Kelly, *The Psychology of Personal Constructs*, 2 vols. (New York: W. W. Norton and Co., 1955). Gregory Bateson, *Steps to an Ecology of Mind* (New York: Ballantine Books, Inc., 1972).
11. Luigi Gedda and Lydia Neroni, "Reazioni posturali e mimiche

di 56 coppie di gemelli alla proiezione di film umoristici ed anziogeni," *Acta Geneticae Medicae et Gemellologiae*, IV (1955), 15–31.

12. Noam Chomsky, "Review of *Verbal Behavior* by B. F. Skinner," *Language*, XXXV (No. 1, 1959), 26–58.

13. "From the History of an Infantile Neurosis" (1918 [1914]), *Std. Ed.*, XVII, 99, 42, and 52.

14. W. W. Meissner, "Freud's Methodology," *Journal of the American Psychoanalytic Association*, XIX (April, 1971), 265–309, 303; "The Operational Principle and Meaning in Psychoanalysis," *Psychoanalytic Quarterly*, XXXV (1966), 233–255, 249, 251.

15. Margaret Mead, *Growing Up in New Guinea* (New York: Mentor Books, 1953), p. vi. Ruth Benedict, *The Chrysanthemum and the Sword* (Boston: Houghton Mifflin Co., 1946). Erik H. Erikson, *Childhood and Society*, 2d ed. (New York: W. W. Norton and Co., 1963), Chapters 3 and 4. Raymond A. Bauer, "Problem Solving Behavior in Organizations: A Functional Point of View," in *Business Policy Cases with Behavioral Science Implications*, ed. Merwin M. Hargrove, Ike H. Harrison, and Eugene Swearingen (Homewood, Ill.: Richard D. Irwin, Inc., 1963). Lucian Pye, *Politics, Personality, and Nation Building: Burma's Search for Identity* (New Haven and London: Yale University Press, 1962). Stanley Hoffman, *Gulliver's Troubles, Or the Setting of American Foreign Policy*, The Atlantic Policy Series (New York: McGraw-Hill Book Co., 1968).

v